TEEN GIRLS ONLY!

DAILY THOUGHTS FOR TEENAGE GIRLS

Text and preface ©2001 by Patricia Hoolihan
Cover woodcut by Rick Allen
Author photograph by William Pringle Rodman

Grateful acknowledgement to Patricia Hoolihan,
Jan Zita Grover, and Lisa McKhann who provided
invaluable editorial assistance.

Library of Congress Cataloging-in-Publication Data

Hoolihan, Patricia
Teen girls only! : daily thoughts for teenage girls/Patricia
Hoolihan.
p. cm.
ISBN 0-930100-31-X
1. Teenage girls—conduct of life. I. Title.
BJ1651.H66 2000
158.1'28'352—dc21   00-063257

First Printing—2001
10 9 8 7 6 5 4 3 2 1

Pulbished by Holy Cow! Press, Post Office Box 3170, Mount
Royal Station, Duluth, Minnesota 55803.
Distributed to the trade by Consortium Book
Sales & Distribution, 1045 Westgate Drive,
Saint Paul, Minnesota 55114.

TEEN GIRLS ONLY!

DAILY THOUGHTS FOR TEENAGE GIRLS

BY

PATRICIA HOOLIHAN

HOLY COW! PRESS • 2001 • DULUTH MINNESOTA

ACKNOWLEDGMENTS

A special thanks to Jim Perlman, publisher of Holy Cow! Press, for giving me the opportunity and support to write this book. Many thanks to Jan Zita Grover, for fine-tuning these pages to a clearer and more perfect pitch.

From the bottom of my heart, thank you to the people who keep me going, as a writer and as a human being, especially my husband, my running friends, and Christine T. Additional thanks to my husband, Chris, and his high school students, who took the time to answer my questionnaire on life as a teenage girl.

Thanks to my friends who went the extra mile to provide me with much-needed source books near the end of this journey, especially Peggy G. and Jennette L.

I want to thank and acknowledge some of the writers who helped provide inspiration for this book. Not only did they help me understand more clearly the issues facing teenage girls today, but also their wise words inspired me and are sprinkled throughout as quotations of the day. Many thanks go to Mary Pipher (*Reviving Ophelia*), Gladys Folkers and Jeanne Engelmann (*Taking Charge of My Mind and Body*), Mindy Morgenstern (*The Real Rules for Girls*), Carmen Renee Berry (*Coming Home to Your Body*), Louise Erdrich, Linda Hogan, Lisel Mueller, Mary Oliver, Ruth Brin, and many others.

For my daughter, Caitlin Rose,
with loving wishes for a safe and exciting
passage through your teen years.

And for my parents, who gracefully
survived my own teen years.

Around the time I was working on the last section of this book, my monthly column was due for the neighborhood newspaper. Right before the deadline, of course, I wrote about watching my 12-year-old daughter perform as a skater to Don McLean's "American Pie," a song popular during my teen years. I wrote: "Music triggers the memory: I feel myself simultaneously as a 17-year-old and as a mother, watching my daughter gliding onto the opening edge of her teen years."

Much of what I've written in this book is a blend between remembering who I was as a teenage girl and watching the teenage girls I know and care about today. I think about my daughter and all of her friends. I watch the girls I have taught in writing classes as they sail through these teen years. In many ways, it is a different world today: girls are faced by difficult issues at a much younger age and at a faster pace. Yet relationship struggles and the need to sort out who and what a teen girl wants to be are parts of a timeless journey.

The teen years can be tumultuous. So much change, so many choices. The years are rich in challenges, opportunities, the lessons of love and fun. My hope is that these meditations will provide inspiration and comfort. I hope they bring gentle reminders to each one of you that your journey is important, special, something to be honored. A couple of times each week, a meditation closes with a writing exercise. These are meant to be fun and interesting and to provide ways to further explore who you are and who you want to be.

May these words, ideas, and images act as a lifeline tossed to you while you sail across the stormy and incredibly exciting seas of your teen years.

JANUARY

I WAKE EXPECTANT, HOPING TO SEE A NEW THING.
-ANNIE DILLARD

I love the first day of the new year. Everything seems possible. My friends and I celebrated last night, throwing confetti and singing and laughing. It was a blast.

There's so much excitement with beginnings. We talked about our goals for the year ahead: what we would like to accomplish, what character traits we want to let go of and what ones we want to develop. I wanted to let go of my tendency to worry and develop listening more because I tend to talk a lot.

Writing exercise: I will write down my goals for the year ahead, the parts of my personality I want to let go of and the parts I want to encourage.

WHAT ARE YOUR SOURCES OF INSPIRATION?

My grandfather, who is in his 70s and still gets out and cross-country skis, inspires me. He loves to ski and when he comes back in, his cheeks are rosy and his spirits are high, even though he's not fast anymore. My uncle, who flies for a living, inspires me because he's found a way to do what he loves and because flying is such an adventure.

People who are really good at what they do inspire me: figure skaters, poets, composers, musicians. When inspiration moves through me, it's like a tidal wave of energy. I'm reminded of what I love and what's important to me. Inspiration comes and goes, but it helps feed the daily work of following my dreams.

Writing exercise: Write about who inspires me and why. I'll describe a moment of inspiration I have felt recently and how it connects to what's important to me.

IF YOU WANT THE TRUTH, I'LL TELL YOU THE TRUTH:
LISTEN TO THE SECRET SOUND, THE REAL SOUND,
WHICH IS INSIDE YOU.
-KABIR

Every once in a while I end up with some quiet time on my hands. My tendency is to want to fill it, but my Mom sometimes makes me just slow down. She says it's important to know how to be alone and quiet. I rarely seek this out, but when it happens, I end up playing the piano or painting or reading. At first, I resist. I feel restless. I try to start an argument with my mother.

But after a while, I begin to feel peaceful. I play a song on the piano that I haven't played in months, and it feels good to remember this song again. Or I find I'm six chapters into a book and way beyond the required four chapters for English next week. Reading, I enter a different, a magical world.

*There is a secret sound inside me I need to
slow down and listen to: it is the true me.*

IF YOU WANT TO KNOW THE MIRACLE,
HOW WIND CAN POLISH A MIRROR
LOOK: THE SHINING GLASS GROWS GREEN IN SPRING.
—GHALIB

When I read these lines in a poetry book, I was struck by the playful images and the word miracle. I think what the poet was saying is that the world is a miraculous place. The force and gentleness of wind are amazing. The wind is powerful enough to polish, well, a mirror. How about a mountain face? Trees that are near open water get permanently bent in the direction that the wind blows.

And there is nothing quite as magical as all the growing green things in spring.

If I want to know the miracle of life, all I have to do is look, really look, all around me.

PINE NEEDLES SING WITH RAIN
AND A NIGHT CRAWLER,
WITH ITS FIVE HEARTS,
BEATS IT
ACROSS THE ROAD.
–LINDA HOGAN

My Aunt Jane spoke with me the other day about how important it is to believe in something bigger and more generous and powerful than we humans. She says a lot of people believe in God, although others use different names: All-Powerful or All-Loving, a Higher Power or Mother Earth, Goodness or The Force or The Universe. There are even more names.

When we pay attention to rain on pine needles or to the amazing life forms all around us, we honor a Creative Force in this world. My aunt says it's important to be grateful for this force, that there is a lot of life to be celebrated in this ever-amazing (though often difficult) world.

Writing exercise: In the next day or two, I will sit down and list ten amazing things I have noticed around me. Then I will write about why I am grateful for them.

EDUCATION IS THE JEWEL CASTING
BRILLIANCE INTO THE FUTURE.
–MARI EVANS

Learning about our world–its literature, history, music, art–is what high school years are about. It's easy to forget this, because we all get distracted with our social life. But what we learn now creates a foundation of knowledge and understanding that we can build on the rest of our lives.

My neighbor says the seeds of her love and interest in writing were planted in high school, and although it took her a while to realize she wanted to be a writer, that's what she is now. She wishes she would have watered those seeds even more back then, but she still remembers teachers who praised and encouraged her work: their words helped her to have courage later in life.

Today I will listen, learn, and pay special attention to what interests me. What I learn today can light up my tomorrow.

LIVE THE QUESTIONS NOW. PERHAPS ONE DISTANT
DAY YOU WILL LIVE INTO THE ANSWERS.
–RAINIER MARIA RILKE

There are so many questions at my age! Who am I? Who are my truest friends? What should or will I become? Who should I hang out with this weekend? I like Jeff, but he wants to see me more often than I want to see him. Why didn't Teresa invite me on her family trip? The unchaperoned party this weekend: what should I do about that?

I like the idea of living the questions. It helps me feel that I don't have to know the answers right now but that the answers may become clear. I think I just have to wrestle with these questions. This may mean mostly thinking about them, or talking with a friend or even an adult. Sometimes writing about things in my journal helps a lot.

Writing exercise: What are the questions in my life right now? I can learn to honor the questions themselves by writing about them, and by imagining answers.

FRIENDS ARE LIKE THE ROOT SYSTEM THAT
HELPS SUPPORT THE TREE OF OUR LIVES.

My good friends are like roots of a tree. They nurture me, nourish me, fertilize me, and help me stand tall. How? By encouraging me to exercise my talents. By encouraging me when I take care of myself. By asking how I am and caring about my answer. By being there for me when I'm going through a rough time. They help me know I'm a good person by enjoying being with me and having fun with me.

A tree whose root system gets injured or sick in some way will eventually topple. Healthy roots make a tree stand tall and beautiful and continue to grow and replenish itself. Choosing friends who are good to me and good for me is very important.

Are my friends providing me with a healthy root system?

STORMY EMOTIONS ARE OFTEN A PART OF THE TEEN YEARS.

I can have a streak of good days or weeks and then, seemingly out of the blue, I will be all out of sorts. I'm crabby, I know I am, but I can't stop myself. Sometimes I say and do things I can't believe I'm doing.

Hormones, my Aunt Jane says. But I think it's more than that. There is a lot I'm trying to figure out: my place with my friends, how to act around boys, especially one I think is special. How to accept myself and like myself, which sports and activities are most important to me. It does help, often a whole lot, to get underneath my crabbiness and think, write, or talk about all this stuff churning inside me.

When I'm behaving in a way that doesn't feel good,
I need to take time to question and to look at what
storm is brewing inside me.

OF WHAT IS FOG THE BEGINNING?
–CARL SANDBURG

The other day when I woke up, the fog outside my window was so thick I could just barely make out my favorite willow tree in the yard. It looked magical and mysterious. When I walked to my bus stop, the moisture licked at my cheeks and made my hair curl a bit. I know it was hard for people driving, but it was great walking in it. My whole world looked different.

Sometimes the weather treats us to special effects. I love how nature can reach inside and calm or soothe or wake me up. We wrote about the fog in my English class and this was a great way to savor the experience, because by afternoon the fog lifted.

Writing exercise: I'll write about how the weather has recently reached inside and touched me in some way.

GESTURES OF GIVING ARE IMPORTANT.

Our high school English class has hooked up with a nearby grade school's fourth grade. Once a week they come over, or we walk over there. And I spend an hour reading with one or two fourth graders.

I have to say this has become one of my favorite times of the week. These kids are hungry for the attention, and it's so much fun both to help them with their reading and to talk about books with them. I feel like I'm "teaching," and it feels great.

If there's a chance to be kind or helpful to a young child around me, taking the time to do that is good for my soul.

EVERY DAY IS A GOD, EACH DAY IS A GOD
AND HOLINESS HOLDS FORTH IN TIME.
–ANNIE DILLARD

I noticed that something special happened to me every day this week. One day my older cousin called and asked me to be in her wedding next summer. I feel so honored to be asked, and I know it will be a blast. Another day I found out that the science project my friend Teresa and I worked on took first place. We worked hard on that for weeks, and it sure feels great to know we did so well.

Another day I passed my next level of skating. Again, it was a moment of triumph after a lot of hard work. Even the days when I didn't have something big happen, I noticed that things were going well with my friends and my family, and I felt grateful.

Writing exercise: I'll list all the good things that have happened to me recently. Then I'll write in detail about one or two of the things for which I feel most grateful.

WHEN THE SHORT DAY IS BRIGHTEST, WITH FROST AND FIRE,
THE BRIEF SUN FLAMES THE ICE, ON POND AND DITCHES,
IN WINDLESS COLD THAT IS THE HEART'S HEAT.
—T.S. ELIOT

Often winter at its darkest and coldest surprises us with a moment of fierce beauty. I walked out of school after a late play rehearsal and felt tired and cold. I knew I still had a lot of homework to do that night. I hadn't worn a hat, and the wind whistled right through my ears. Then I looked up and saw the full moon rising, shining through the black leafless branches.

It was so beautiful I almost gasped. For a moment, I stopped and just let that beauty enter me. It made me wonder if most of life's hard moments might not carry some moment of beauty or insight or kindness, if I only stop to notice.

I will look for moments that warm my heart,
especially when life feels cold or hard.

I HAVE A DREAM THAT ONE DAY THIS NATION WILL RISE
UP AND LIVE OUT THE TRUE MEANING OF ITS CREED:
WE HOLD THESE TRUTHS TO BE SELF-EVIDENT,
THAT ALL MEN ARE CREATED EQUAL.
–MARTIN LUTHER KING, JR.

If written today, the Constitution of the United States would read men and women (at least since women won the right to vote). In history I am learning that as females, we have a long history of fighting for such basic rights, as do minorities in our country. When I think about my female ancestors not being allowed to vote, I'm outraged. When I think about black people being made to sit at the back of the bus, I feel the same way.

Our history teacher says we are all either part of the solution or part of the problem, that it's important for each one of us to fight against the unfair and inaccurate cultural stereotypes we may carry inside us and to reach beyond them.

Writing exercise: I will write about one or two stereotypes I have in my head and then explore ways to break them through action, reading, or talking with a trusted adult.

IT'S THE ROSE'S UNFOLDING, GHALIB,
THAT CREATES THE DESIRE TO SEE—
IN EVERY COLOR AND CIRCUMSTANCE,
MAY THE EYES BE OPEN FOR WHAT COMES.
—GHALIB

Roses are my absolutely favorite flowers. There are so many layers to them, wrapped at first tightly around their core. When they begin to open, I'm always amazed by how many petals are unfurling. And the smell! Breathe deep, and it just makes you feel good. When a rose begins to droop and I peel the petals away, I remember all over again how there is nothing softer than the inside of a rose petal.

I think the desire to see is what makes a vibrant life. I know some people who have little desire to see the rose or much else in this world. They dull their senses with drugs and smother themselves in unhappiness.

*I will live my life with vibrancy, seeing
what is in front of me with clear eyes.*

A REPUTATION IS A VALUABLE COMMODITY: PROTECT IT.

Martin Luther King, Jr. wrote that the most important thing in life is developing character. Character seems to be a complex mix of honesty, integrity and respect for oneself and others. I hear a lot about how hardship can build character, but with some people, hardship hardens or weakens them.

Character determines our reputation. If we are honest and respectful to people, our reputation will grow strong. A bad reputation, once acquired, is a hard thing to shake.

By developing my character (my morals, values,
and integrity), I build a strong and positive reputation.
This is important to have.

WE ARE ALL TRIBUTARIES FEEDING THE RIVER OF LIFE.

In science class we learned how the fluttering of a butterfly's wings in South America can affect wind patterns all over the globe. Such intricate and far-reaching interconnections amazed me. It made me think about how last year's crabby English teacher affected all of us so differently from this year's English teacher, who makes learning fun and makes all of us feel special.

The other morning I passed my elderly neighbor on the sidewalk, and I was so focused on my own problems that I barely said hello. Then I saw this flash of disappointment cross her face. I realized that instead of brightening her day, I had brought a shadow to it. Next time, I'll be more sensitive to how my actions affect people around me.

*Writing exercise: I'll list some of the ways I have made
life brighter for people around me in the last few days.
Then I'll list other things I can do in the days ahead.*

·WE ALL HAVE QUESTIONS ABOUT SEXUALITY.

When the subject of sex comes up, none of us can believe our parents ever do it. This makes us all laugh. The lucky ones among us can talk about sexuality with our parents, but even so, it's a little awkward. Still, I have found that when I really need information or have some questions, my parents do know a lot. Lindsay's cousin got pregnant at 17, and she said it was with a guy she didn't even like all that well. And now her whole life will be affected by this.

Being responsible for my body includes gathering all the information I can and being thoughtful about my goals. As my Aunt Jane says, being sexual carries a big price tag: complex emotional ties (maybe more than I can handle at my age), risk of disease, risk of pregnancy, risk of hurting my reputation.

!

I need to think about what I do with my body.
It's helpful to talk with my friends, but I may
also need some adult guidance.

OUR BODIES, OUR SELVES.

My friends and I have been talking lately about our bodies. About being in charge of our bodies. One of our friends, Alison, had an awful experience: a guy reached out on a crowded city bus and grabbed her. She pulled away and cried out, and although no one around really knew what he'd done, enough people looked up that he moved away. She said she felt really scared and icky afterwards.

We talked a lot about being smart and protecting our bodies. Sometimes this means not being out alone at night in questionable or unsafe places. It means choosing boys who are safe and trustworthy. It means not putting ourselves in risky situations, like drinking at unsupervised parties.

When I protect my body, I protect my heart and soul as well.

DO NOT COMPARE YOURSELF TO OTHERS,
FOR ALWAYS THERE WILL BE THOSE
GREATER AND LESSER THAN YOURSELF.
—DESIDERATA

When I'm having a bad day, everybody around me looks more talented, smarter, and luckier than I am. Lindsay plays the piano better than I do. Teresa is a better soccer player. Hannah gets straight As with hardly even trying. Jessica's family has a lot more money than we do.

When I focus on such things, I put myself down. On a better day, I realize all that I have. My body is healthy, and I'm a pretty good athlete myself. I can sing and dance and play many songs on the piano, even though I haven't been taking lessons as long as Lindsay has. I'm energetic and adventurous, and I like this in me, and so do my friends.

I'll avoid comparing myself to others and focus on what I like about me and my life.

COMPASSION IS AN IMPORTANT QUALITY
TO HAVE IN THIS WORLD.

Compassion, says my mother, humbles me and connects me to others. I have a couple of friends right now whom I feel much compassion for. Cassie's parents are divorcing, and she's so upset. I've noticed she cries easily and looks distracted a lot of the time. It's taking Lizzie a long time to build her strength back up after her pneumonia, and this is hard for her. Lindsay's boyfriend just broke up with her and is already with somebody else, and she's feeling really sad about that.

I ask them how they are and listen a lot. I know that when I'm going through a rough time, they will do the same for me. I'm finding that I need support, too, in order to better support my friends who are struggling.

Today I am noticing the network of caring in my life.

AMAZING GRACE, HOW SWEET THE SOUND . . .

The root word for grace is gratus, which means pleasing or grateful. There are twenty-one entries in the Oxford English Dictionary under the noun grace and five more entries under grace as a verb. I recently read somewhere that grace and gratitude are intimately connected.

When I appreciate what I have, life feels more abundant. There was an article in the paper last week about people who see the glass as half full and others who see it as half empty . . . . even though there's the same amount in the glass. Optimists live longer and healthier lives than people who are more negative.

I can be more of a glass-is-half-full person
by being grateful for everything I have.

WHO MADE THE WORLD?
WHO MADE THE SWAN, AND THE BLACK BEAR?
–MARY OLIVER

The world is an amazing place. Every once in a while I stop to wonder and ask questions about the tree in front of my house or the existence of black holes. How is it that the stars move so methodically that we can plot where we are on earth and what time of year it is by their location?

Another amazing thing is that some animals move in response to the stars and sun. Snakes and bears know when to prepare for hibernation without ever having studied the seasons. All of life is interconnected, and one way I honor my connection is by noticing, wondering about, and admiring everything around me.

Writing exercise: I will write a page of questions about the amazing world I live in. I could start with who made the bird out my window? How does it sing so beautifully?

When one door closes, another opens.

My older brother was playing basketball and swimming last year when he fell and hurt his leg badly. He ended up being unable to play basketball for an entire season, but swimming helped his body regain its strength.

He was really bummed, but the truth is, it was hard to do justice to both sports. He was having a hard time choosing between the two. I overheard my Dad saying it was a blessing in disguise, and swimming suits my brother's personality much better. This year, my brother is winning all sorts of swimming awards. His energy and time aren't split between the two sports and so he's more focused.

Sometimes when a door closes in my life, I need to look around for where another door is opening.

WELL, MAYBE WE COULD ALL USE A LITTLE GRACE.
TO KNOW WHEN TO RUN AND
WHEN TO STAY IN ONE PLACE.
–SHERYL CROW

Sometimes I wonder if I should walk away from a friendship or an activity that isn't going well. Or should I hang in and be patient through a tough phase? How to know what to do? How to figure it out?

Sheryl Crow sings about grace, and my aunt says grace comes by opening ourselves to it, it can't be forced. She has read a lot about a saint from the Middle Ages who defined grace as a gift that flows from God. In the flowing, it heals or nourishes or comforts us. My aunt says grace (whether you call it prayer or slowing down or meditation), often comes in quiet moments. But she says it also comes in other ways: magical moments are all around us, waiting for us to notice.

*If I'm feeling confused or stuck, I will slow down
and ask for a moment of grace to flow into me,
so I can clearly see what I need to do.*

I'M IN CHARGE OF THE EFFORT, NOT THE RESULT.

I work hard at a lot of things: schoolwork, soccer, skating. When it comes time for a game, a competition, or grades, the results don't always seem fair to me. There's a soccer ref who makes bad calls, judges at a competition seem off in their judging, or a teacher seems like he's grading really low.

These are parts of my life I do not have control over. But I do have control over the effort that goes into my activities. When I know I've prepared well and done my best, then I feel better. Trying to get by without being prepared is not a good feeling.

I need to take charge in my life where I can.

CONFLICT HAPPENS—I NEED TO FIND
HEALTHY WAYS TO DEAL WITH IT.

When water boils, it either has to be turned down, or the lid taken off, or it will spill over onto the stove. When I'm mad at someone, it feels like I'm boiling inside. Usually the feelings build slowly to a boil. But sometimes the heat of anger builds up fast.

If I don't find a way to take the lid off or turn the heat down, this anger spills across my life. Then I'm crabby and short-tempered about everything. But when I actually talk my anger over—for instance, when I tell my mom what she did that made me so mad, or I tell Beth that her not calling me made me mad—it's like taking the lid off. Talking to the person I'm angry with helps turn the heat down on my anger in a healthy way.

Conflict is a part of relationships. Talking about it respectfully is a good way to turn the heat of anger down.

What about money and desire?

In social science we studied commercials and the power and seductiveness of TV and magazine, catalogue, and billboard ads. It was an eye-opener. These ads are meant to make us want things–to desire things we might not think about otherwise. This is why my neighbor's mother has never let her watch anything other than public TV.

There's always something I want to buy. I earn my own spending money, though, and I'm supposed to be saving some of it. If I bought everything I wanted, I'd have to borrow money to do it. Studying these ads made me angry: suddenly I didn't want to be a puppet at the end of an advertiser's string. I had never thought about my buying and spending in such a way.

If I find myself wanting too much–for instance, more than I can afford–maybe I'm being too influenced by commercials. I need to be thoughtful about spending and saving money.

I CAN START OVER AS MANY TIMES AS I NEED TO.

I heard a story the other day about an Olympic cross-country skier. When she first took off from the starting gate, with tons of spectators and TV cameras watching, she fell. Most people watching were horrified. This is a sport where every tenth of a second counts.

But she picked herself up quickly and got going again.

She didn't give up, didn't even think about giving up. When I think about the same thing happening to me, I wonder if I would have just given up. I hope not. That kind of feisty, I-can-start-over-again spirit is something I admire and want to have. (By the way, she skied into first place.)

Falls, mistakes, disappointments don't have to stop me. I can always start over again.

> To Ojibwe speakers the language is a deeply
> loved entity. There is a spirit or an
> originating genius belonging to each word.
> —Louise Erdrich

Language has such power: the power to heal, to remember, to connect human beings with each other. The Ojibwes believe that each word in their language has spirit. The very idea makes me stop and think and appreciate words. It also makes me think about how many languages there are now and have been over the centuries.

Why am I attracted to certain words? Are other people attracted to other words? What might the sound and meaning and spirit of a word in another language have to teach me?

Writing exercise: I want to write five of my favorite words down and then create a story or poem using all of them. Why, right now in my life, am I attracted to these words?

THERE WILL ALWAYS BE PEOPLE WHO WILL RIDE
WITH YOU IN THE LIMOUSINE, BUT WHAT YOU WANT
IS SOMEONE WHO'LL TAKE THE BUS WITH YOU
WHEN THE LIMO BREAKS DOWN.
–OPRAH WINFREY

Sometimes people choose friends based on what others can do for them or give to them. Jessica's family has a lot of money, and girls flock to her because she always has a car and because she gets to throw parties often. Everyone wants to be invited.

I like knowing my friends are choosing me because of me, not because of what I have to offer. I want to be liked and appreciated and for who I am. That's also how I want to choose my friends.

True friendship is based on liking and respecting each other.

FEBRUARY

A TIME FOR REMEMBERING, A TIME FOR FORGETTING.
–Ecclesiastes

Sometimes I am so impatient! I want my mother's attention right now. I want my brother to go away right now. I want to pass my test right now.

Patience means accepting that there is a time for everything and that it may not be right now. A time to live, a time to die, a time for anger, a time for forgiveness. Certain feelings and cycles in life and in relationships cannot be rushed. A time for family, a time for friends. I want to slow down enough so I can pay attention to what the time is right for today. I want to be a more patient person.

Writing exercise: I'll write about time.
What is it time for right now in my life, and what is
it not time for? How can I practice patience today?

BOYS ADD A LOT OF FUN AND CONFUSION TO MY LIFE.

My friends and I are just starting to hang out more with boys. There are more dances now and things like that. Some of us are already dating; some of us have been dating for a while. I find the world of dating sort of complicated. I'll get a crush on a boy and then wonder if he likes me. Then I'll start to talk with him a lot, and if we decide to go out, it can be a lot of fun.

But do I call him? Wait for him to call me? What about when I can tell somebody else likes the same guy I do? What I like best is doing things in a group of boys and girls. I'm glad I have my best friend, Lizzie, so we can talk all this over. Even my older brother is occasionally helpful.

What place does a specific boy or boys have in my life right now? This may be a good question to talk over with a close friend, a trusted adult, or my journal.

WHAT IS RESPONSIBLE USE?

Sooner or later I'm going to be faced with decisions about drinking and using drugs. When we had the DARE (Drug and Alcohol Resistance Education) program at school, we talked about ways to say no–creative ways, so we wouldn't feel stuck or trapped or forced to do something we weren't comfortable doing.

My father is a recovering alcoholic, and on both sides of my family are more alcoholics. I have a cousin who's wasted his life on drugs. My mom says I have to realize that I have a genetic predisposition toward addiction. Studies show over and over again that genes play a role. She says my body is way too young right now to handle the power of drinking or drugs and that, even when I'm older, I will need to be cautious and remember my history.

When faced with the choice about drinking,
I need to consider many factors: my genetic history,
my age, the fact that it's illegal when I'm involved
in sports, and that I'm legally underage.

Do you not see the sun above the wall
Sinks to nothing this evening
emerges anew tomorrow?
–Pao Chao (421-465 C.E.)

Tonight is Chinese New Year's Eve. At my friend Lee's house, they are celebrating with all sorts of Chinese food her mother has been busy making. Lee has been telling me about her favorite: a tray of sweetmeats called Chuen-Hop, which means "tray of togetherness." Watermelon seeds symbolize having plenty. My friends and I are invited. There will be music and dancing, and I can't wait.

Close to midnight all the children will be given red envelopes with good-luck money inside. It is called Lai-See. Around this same time all the young people bow and pay their respects to the parents and elders. I am intrigued by this conscious celebration of the older ones and the focus on being grateful and celebrating life.

*Even if I'm not Chinese, I can take this day to honor
the older and wiser people in my life and
to be grateful for all that I have.*

TODAY IS CHINESE NEW YEAR.

In China, spring is beginning. Here, it is winter. Our planet is a balanced place of opposites. In art class today we painted the Chinese calendar. Each month and year is represented by an animal. I was born in the year of the Rabbit, an idea I like, because I think rabbits are very gentle animals.

I like the idea of animals representing and expressing who we are and guarding and protecting us. My brother was born in the year of the dragon. Maybe that's why he is so good at expressing his anger—that is, breathing fire.

Writing exercise: I'll write about an animal I have seen or dreamed or thought about recently. What is it about this animal that interests me? How is it like or unlike me?

I HAVE EVERYTHING I NEED.

My mother, my Aunt Jane, and my Sunday School teacher have all talked recently about gratitude, about appreciating what we have. This is something I need to work on, I know. My dad often points that out to me.

It's so easy to always want something more: a new pair of jeans, the latest CD, makeup, friends to sleep over, a bigger bedroom. Thanking can take the place of wanting. But for me, this requires effort. When my class did some community service with poor people in our city, it opened my eyes to how lucky I am and how much I have. I try to think about the bigger picture like this. And I try, at least once a day, to replace wanting with thanking.

Every day I can take a moment to be thankful for all the things and loved ones I have and enjoy.

MANY FEARS ARE BORN OF FATIGUE AND LONELINESS.
–DESIDERATA

Sometimes, when the world seems the darkest, I realize how tired I am. I get crabby. I don't like my life. I don't like my family. I am afraid that my friends like everybody else better than they like me. I don't like me. My dad tells me it's like trying to run a car on an empty gas tank.

The thing is, I forget about how being tired affects me and instead I take everything very personally. Problems feel insurmountable. But if I get a good night's sleep or two, I tend to feel renewed and whatever problems I have seem more manageable.

If I'm feeling afraid or lonely, I can renew myself through sleep or slowing down.

THIS LITTLE LIGHT OF MINE, I'M GOING TO LET IT SHINE.

The other day my little brother was in his room singing this song. It sounded so sweet. Then I heard him telling our mom that one day when he was singing it, he imagined God coming in through the window to hug him. This really made me smile.

And it made me think about letting my light shine. What might that mean? Maybe that I let the best part of me (the part of me that God or an angel or the Great Spirit would want to hug) come out into the light. The best part of me is kind and thoughtful and generous. The best part of me cares about the people in my family and in the world as much as I care about me. The best part of me exercises my talents and abilities.

Writing exercise: I will write the song lyrics at the top of this page. Then I'll write a list of specific ways I can and do let my light shine.

THERE ARE MANY DIFFERENT KINDS OF FAMILIES.

One of my best friends, Ellie, lives alone with her mom. Her parents split up when she was really little, and her father lives in Florida. She goes to visit him every summer. I sometimes envy the simplicity of Ellie's family life and how she and her mom seem to get along so well. They have a very cozy little house. And she doesn't have any little brother to put up with.

Ellie loves to come over to my house. She gets a kick out of my dad, and she thinks my little brother is cute; I think she thinks my older brother is cute, too. Among our classmates, there are many different family situations. Amy has two moms; Claire lives with her dad. I think there is no right way to have a family. What matters most is the love and care in the family.

Families come in many different forms.
What's really important in any family is how
its members love and support each other.

LEARN TO ACCEPT DISAPPOINTMENTS WITH GRACE.

My mom is always saying to me, "I know this is hard, but I also know you can handle it gracefully. When you look back on this later and it doesn't seem as big as it does now, you'll want to look at your behavior and know it was graceful."

Maurya didn't make varsity soccer this year. Jenny didn't get the lead in the school play. My friend Annie is two levels ahead of me in piano. I think being graceful means not turning sour or resenting the ones who got what they wanted this time. I watched Jenny congratulate the girl who got the lead, and she stayed in the play and had fun with her smaller part. I really admired her for those reasons.

Handling disappointment is a challenging but necessary part of life. I can learn to handle my disappointments gracefully.

ALREADY THE LEAVES HAVE SWIRLED
OVER, THE WIND HAS SPOKEN.
–MARY OLIVER

Sometimes, if I listen, it's as if the universe is talking to me. I've had a gentle breeze help calm me and a strong wind energize me just when I needed each one of those qualities. Or I've opened a book and what I've read has given me a helpful idea about a problem I've been wrestling with for days.

A line of music on the radio may comfort me in an unexpected way. Or what a teacher says enters me and helps me in some way. I notice that if I listen and pay attention, even when I'm not looking for anything specific, these small gifts come to me.

*Writing exercise: I'll write about a time
when the world around me offered just what
I needed to hear when I wasn't expecting it.*

ALL NIGHT THEY HAD THOUGHT
OF WHAT THEY WOULD LIKE
THEIR LIVES TO BE, AND IMAGINED
THEIR STRONG, THICK WINGS.
—MARY OLIVER

Imagine wings for flight. Imagine a brain ready for a difficult exam. Imagine a body poised to kick the soccer ball right where it needs to go. Imagine a body and heart ready to sing and dance in the school play. Imagine a world where everyone lives together in peace and harmony.

Imagining the kind of world I want to live in and the kind of person I want to be helps me to feel these are possible. I've noticed that I tend to do better at all sorts of things when I imagine myself doing well.

I will take time today to imagine
the best-hearted self I can be.

THE FLOWER THAT FOLLOWS THE SUN
DOES SO EVEN ON CLOUDY DAYS.
–ROBERT LEIGHTON

Shamrock plants open their blossoms every morning when the sun warms the hills and close every evening when the sun goes down. Fields of sunflowers face east in the morning and turn their faces all day toward the sun; they're facing west by evening. These flowers respond to the sun even when it's hidden behind a thick cloud cover.

Like a growing flower, I follow my dreams and goals. They shine the light of promise. Even on days when my dreams and goals seem far away or dim, I can take small steps toward them.

What I do each day is a part of who I am becoming.

AND THE GRINCH'S SMALL HEART
GREW THREE SIZES THAT DAY
AND THE MINUTE HIS HEART DIDN'T FEEL QUITE SO TIGHT
HE WHIZZED WITH HIS LOAD THROUGH
THE BRIGHT MORNING LIGHT.
–DR. SEUSS

Valentine's Day is a day for remembering love. This year I don't have a special boy in my life, but maybe next year I will. I think Valentine's Day is about a lot more than just that kind of love. My mother always gives me a special card, and so do my grandmothers, reminding me how much they love me. I am one of the loves of their lives, and this makes me feel really special.

Who are the loves of my life? My family and my friends and special teachers. This year I spent the weekend before Valentine's Day making heart cards for all the loves in my life. My heart grew three sizes just making these cards, and then one more size when I gave them away and saw everyone's eyes light up.

Writing exercise: Valentine's Day is a perfect time to write cards to the people I love and am loved by.

WHEN, AFTER HEAVY RAIN, THE STORM CLOUDS DISPERSE,
IS IT NOT THAT THEY'VE WEPT THEMSELVES
CLEAR TO THE END?
—GHALIB

Sometimes for no huge reason, except maybe I'm tired or don't feel well or things didn't go well all day, I just need to cry. Other times I have bigger reasons to cry. I cried when I heard that Julia's dad had died of cancer and I cried again at his funeral. I cried when my cat died on the floor of my bedroom.

It isn't always easy to feel okay about crying or even to let myself do it. But I always feel good afterward. It's like the release after a storm. All those winds of confusion, sadness or disappointment blow through me and then I feel cleansed, more ready to face what's ahead.

*When I need to, I can always cry. A good cry refreshes
my soul like a spring rain refreshes the air and earth.*

BALANCE IS IMPORTANT.

I tend to be hyper. It's hard for me to balance my need for activity and socializing with my need to do quieter things. I almost always choose action over quiet, but if I go nonstop, I often get sick. My friend Ellie is a homebody. She has to push herself to get involved in activities. She loves to read on the couch or practice her piano.

We're good for each other. I push her to get out and do things and she reminds me it's okay to slow down. I need this balance in other ways, too: between family time and friend time; between time with my boyfriend and time with girlfriends; between schoolwork and fun time.

Balance helps me stay on top of my life.

THE STRONGEST CLAY POT IS THE CENTERED POT.

Have you ever seen a potter center clay on a potter's wheel and magically form a perfect pot from it? I've tried centering a lump of clay and it's hard! I had to focus all my attention right between my hands.

Some of the people I admire the most are what I would call centered. They seem to know themselves and their values, and they are naturally themselves–not self-conscious or show-offy. My dad says that these people probably spend a little bit of time every day remembering who they are.

Quiet time helps a person stay clear and centered. Some people call quiet time meditation. Others call it prayer time. (Is it coincidence that strong pots and prayers come out of clasped hands?) When I spend some quiet time–reading, writing in my journal, playing the piano for fun, painting–I can feel a peaceful strength in my bones.

When I take time to be quiet and alone,
I am building my inner strength and center.

WE ALL NEED SOURCES FOR FINDING COMFORT.

Do you remember that best-selling book from a few years ago, *When Bad Things Happen to Good People*? I never read the book, but I love the title, and just the words of it help me from time to time. There was one week around here when we found out my aunt had breast cancer and then my dad had a minor car accident that hurt his arm, and I fell down the back steps and sprained my ankle.

"What's wrong with us?" haunted me until I remembered that title. Hard and bad things do happen, and it doesn't mean there's something wrong with me or my family. It does mean I need to look for comfort—from my parents, good friends, music, or whatever Greater Power I believe in.

Writing exercise: When bad things happen,
what are my sources of comfort?
I'll write about what comforts and soothes me.

LET PEACE BEGIN WITH ME.

A big fight broke out at our school the other day. It was between black kids and Asian kids. You could feel the tension in the whole school for days afterward. Several students were suspended. Many of us were upset.

I sometimes wonder why it's so hard for everybody to get along, why there is always a war going on somewhere. My history teacher says we all have prejudices and it's important to examine them, question them, stretch ourselves beyond them. I don't want to be the kind of person who responds to others based on the color of their skin or the look of their clothes.

I want to be a source of peace in this world, not prejudice.
I can do this by responding to people's character,
not their looks, and by developing my own character.

MY PARENTS AREN'T PERFECT.

One of the things I am slowly learning is how to talk to my mom or dad when I'm upset with them. In the past, I have tended to become very unfriendly and untalkative. But my dad is pretty good at asking me what's wrong often enough and in a nice enough way that I finally talk.

Last week I told my dad I was upset that he didn't keep his promise to put up my new bookshelves. I told my mom that when she gets so busy that she isn't around at all in the evenings, I feel unimportant. It helped to say both of those things, and my parents listened and understood, and then I felt better.

*I'm learning that it helps to talk when I'm upset
rather than hold my feelings close and tight.*

I NEED GOOD LUCK.

Good luck comes and it goes, but I like to find ways to encourage its arrival. I collect good-luck items. On my homework desk, I have smooth, dark-blue rocks from my favorite summer beach. I have a carved fairy a friend brought me from Ireland. My mother gave me a pendant that is very old and smooth from my grandmother. Sometimes I just like to pick it up and rub it in my hands and think about the women who have worn it.

My good-luck items always come from places and people I care about. Maybe they are mostly symbols of love and positive energy. The important thing is, they make me feel good. They make me feel lucky.

What other good-luck reminders
can I incorporate into my life?

SINCE YOU ARE LIKE NO OTHER BEING EVER CREATED
SINCE THE BEGINNING OF TIME, YOU ARE INCOMPARABLE.
–BRENDA UELAND

There is nobody in the world like me! Nobody in the world with this exact blend of talents and thinking and interests and energy and looks. I am an individual. I respond to the world in my own way. It is never a good idea to expect myself to be or to act or to think like other people. And this is good! This is a thing to be celebrated!

I can cut my own trail. I don't have to narrow or shrink myself to fit in. If I have the courage and strength to be my own person, I'll have more fun and a more vital life and I will be more interesting!

Go, girl, sing your own tune!

IN A DARK TIME, THE EYE BEGINS TO SEE.
–THEODORE ROETHKE

Two years ago, our family went through a rough couple of months. The same month my dad moved out, my uncle became terminally sick. My dad moved back in, but my uncle died. That was a very dark time.

I knew my mom and dad weren't getting along, and I desperately wanted their marriage to improve, which it did eventually. It was so sad watching my uncle and his children suffer. But I learned a lot about the power of love in a family and about who my true friends were. I learned a lot about how to cope with and work my way through a dark time. Friendship, music, skating, and prayer were the flames that lit my way.

*Writing exercise: I'll write about a dark time and what
the small flames were that lit up my darkness.*

THERE ARE HUNDREDS OF WAYS TO
KNEEL AND KISS THE GROUND.
–RUMI

Kissing the ground is a way to be thankful for the earth we live, eat, drive, play, and love each other on. There are many other ways to love and be thankful for this earth. Indians pray and worship the earth. A friend of my aunt is a dancer, and she likes to walk slowly, allowing herself to feel the earth beneath her feet. My father's best friend works for environmental issues all the time.

We can plant trees, pick up litter, bike or walk instead of driving. We can enjoy and be thankful daily for earth's stunning beauty. The earth is our home, a home that needs to be loved and care for.

*Writing exercise: What are some of the ways
I can honor and celebrate the earth?*

I ACCEPT MYSELF AS IMPERFECT.

I'm attracted to the idea of perfection the way I am to a lake on a perfectly calm day. When a lake is absolutely still, it's easy to forget how recently it was alive with waves and whitecaps.

Perfection is about as permanent as a perfectly still, reflective lake. I need to remember that it's a worthy goal, and to enjoy the times when life is going perfectly. But I also need to remember that it's the times when life seems stormy that teach me the most and that are perhaps the richest. They're like the turnover in a lake, which brings all the bottom richness up to the surface.

Instead of being hard on myself for not being perfect,
I'll celebrate the strength that gets me through hard times.

THERE ARE SOME FEARS THAT GO ALONG WITH BEING FEMALE IN OUR WORLD TODAY.

Ever since I was a little girl, my parents have been very protective about me walking anywhere too far by myself. They have always limited how far I can walk with friends, especially at night. My mom says she feels sorry for my generation; there wasn't this kind of fear when she was a child. She was freer to roam the neighborhood.

This just seems to be part of my reality. It makes me grateful for the places I do feel safe: my home (locked), my friends' houses, school. Our summer vacation place feels especially safe.

Occasionally I need to talk about these feelings.
I also try to savor the times and places where I feel safe.

IT'S AWKWARD BUT IMPORTANT TO TALK ABOUT GETTING MY PERIOD.

Being able to talk about having my period is helpful. I sometimes talk with my mom, especially when I have questions about what products to use. My friends and I talk about the challenges of having our period during a ski meet or a soccer competition. Some of us have more pain than others, and some have a heavier flow. One friend is very irregular and others of us are very regular.

It helps to talk and not feel alone with this part of my life. It also helps to read books, to know what's normal and what might mean we should go to a doctor. Even though it feels a little awkward to talk about my periods, I'm glad I have a mom I can go to with my questions.

Talking about menstruation with other girls can be comforting, informative, helpful, and even fun. It's well worth any initial awkwardness.

DREAMS AND DISCIPLINE GO TOGETHER.

One of my dreams is to go to a really good college. I talk with my dad about this a lot. He says that dreams are like the mountain top and a whole lot of small steps and training precede the climb. He says discipline is a key part of reaching my dream.

When I talk about this dream, my dad says, "Study hard. Never settle for less than the best you can do. Do well in other activities, too, because colleges want a well rounded person." So, I drew a mountain top and painted it and wrote the college of my dreams on it, and I know when I'm at my desk studying or writing a paper that I'm climbing toward my dream.

Writing exercise: I'll write a list of my dreams.
For each dream, I'll write what steps I need to be taking
now and in the next months or years in order to reach it.

HOW I WOULD PAINT
THE LEAP OF FAITH:

A BLACK CAT JUMPING UP THREE FEET
TO REACH A THREE-INCH SHELF.
–LISEL MUELLER

Leap Day. Leap Year. I sometimes think about the people who figured out calendars and how to keep track of the passage of time. It must have required leaps of adventurous and daring thinking along with the ability to imagine beyond the easily visible.

A leap of faith. When Cassie's parents split up, she had to work at believing she would be okay no matter what. When I broke up with Brian, I needed to have that blind faith that I could still love life even if I was giving up a boyfriend. When there's a step I need to take, even though I don't know what lies beyond it, that's when I need to have faith in what I can't yet see.

When life requires a leap of faith on my part, let me prepare well, leap fully, and believe in the best.

March

SLOWING DOWN ONCE IN A WHILE IS
GOOD FOR BODY, MIND, AND SOUL.

I was recently sick with strep throat and spent two days on the couch with a fever. My mom was great, and she and I had some good conversations. I also dreamed up ideas for rearranging my room, and when I felt better, I did some reading. I napped where the sun streams into our rec room.

Although I felt weak and I hated to miss school, the slowing down part felt peaceful. Most of my friends and I are very busy. There's homework and sports and band and lots of different activities. My mom says I need to build more quiet time into my life so I don't have to get sick in order to take it. I'm experimenting with this: all week I've lit candles in my room and written in my journal or just closed my eyes and listened to beautiful music. A peaceful feeling comes over me. I like it a lot.

*Slowing down time is an important way
to center myself peacefully.*

March

THERE IS AN ART TO CHOOSING FRIENDS.

So many ingredients go into friendship: similar interests, an ability to have fun with each other, mutual support, and more. My grade school was small and there weren't that many choices, but now there are.

I've been thinking about this, and what's important to me is to have friends who accept me for who I am but who encourage me to be the best I can be. Some of my friends and I compete for best grades and in this way we help each other do our best. I love having friends who use their talents both artistically and athletically and who study hard. I also like having friends who are kind and considerate.

I need to take time to think about what's important to me in friendships. Does this change over time?

WE ALL NEED SOMETHING TO BELIEVE IN.

My grandmother is very religious and goes to church almost every day. Whenever I ask her about the hard times in her life, she tells me it is her faith that helped her through. She always believed God was there, helping her.

One friend's grandmother hosts powwows at her farm and lights candles every day to the Great Spirit. Her awareness of this Great Spirit infuses all her actions. The mother of another friend says she has a hard time with the word God but she adds another *o* to it and uses the idea of goodness as a source of comfort and inspiration.

There are many ways to believe or to have faith
in this world: for most of us, there is comfort in believing
in a force larger than ourselves that works for us.

WHAT ARE THE THINGS I LOVE TO DO?

My teen years are supposed to be a great time for trying out lots of interests. My mom says that some of the things she began in high school have been lifelong passions for her, such as running and piano playing and cross-country skiing.

I have a lot of interests: skating, theatre, soccer, painting, piano, and others. My friend Lindsay, who loves theatre, is in every play and is trying out for assistant director. Karla has entered every art show at school and at the annual summer fair, and she always places. I can see a difference in my school between those who pursue their passions and those who don't seem to care. I want to be one of the vibrant ones.

*Writing exercise: What are the activities in my life
I feel most passionate about? I'll make a list and then
write about the feelings each activity brings out in me.*

SICKNESS CAN HELP US SEE SOME THINGS MORE CLEARLY.

Last week my mother was sick. Really sick. High fevers, very weak, a throat so sore she could hardly talk. Two things happened to me: I realized how much she does for me, and I realized how much I can do for her.

I helped out a lot with my younger brother and with cooking. I brought her tea and soup. She appreciated my help so much, and it felt good to be so needed. When I missed all her little touches, I realized all the things she does in a week for me. Now she's almost back to full steam, but I'm hoping I remember to appreciate what she does for me and that anything I do to help makes a difference.

Helping out in a family is a two-way street: it's important to appreciate the help I receive and to do my share of helping.

TO SMOKE OR NOT TO SMOKE?

In health class we spent a week on cigarette smoking. We read lots of studies on the effects of first- and secondhand smoke. We read statistics on the percent of each age group that smokes. We even did an anonymous poll of our school.

I wonder why smoking looks so cool when it's so bad for you? I wonder why so many people do it when everyone knows it's a health hazard? I don't need to be judgmental about people who do smoke, but it often makes me feel sad. My uncle, who is in his thirties, says he just quit, and it was the hardest thing he's ever done. He really wishes he never started.

It's important at my age to think of the long-term consequences of habits I'm exploring.

LOOK BENEATH THE MEANNESS.

I sometimes find myself being mean. This most often happens at home, toward my mother or my brothers. But sometimes I act this way with my friends. Once, when I was being really bad at home, my mother sent me to my room for an hour and told me to write in my journal about how I was feeling inside.

I fought this idea by polishing my nails first. But then my journal beckoned to me, and I began to write. What came out in my writing surprised me. I was feeling slighted by my mother, as if she cared more about my brothers than me. I was also feeling bad about Andrea spending more time with Ellie than me.

*Acting with meanness toward others may signal that
I need to look at unhappiness within me. I need to be
responsible for my feelings in a direct, not a mean, way.*

I NEED A LITTLE INNOCENCE IN MY LIFE.

Sometimes it feels like high school is not an innocent place. There's a lot of exploration going on. There are drugs and drinking available to those who want it. We're all trying to figure out who we are physically, sexually, and in relationship to the opposite sex. Some kids are dealing with very heavy family problems.

When I feel overwhelmed by these things, it helps to write in my journal or talk with my best friend, my dad, or my favorite aunt. Another thing that helps is the innocent time I spend with kids. The other day I was babysitting, and I took the kids sledding. Snow was falling gently on the trees and our faces, and we flew down the hill, laughing all the way, over and over again. It felt great!

Writing exercise: I need moments of innocence to balance out the harder things in life. I'll write about possible ways of finding innocent moments.

I CAN SEEK MOMENTS OF HARMONY.

Last week was a rough week at our high school. A girl in the junior class tried to commit suicide. There was a big fight in the halls one morning that was race-related. You could feel the tension in the building—all of us were a bit on edge.

In art class we were working on watercolors. Not only did the art teacher let us talk about how we were affected by these events, but she also encouraged us to paint it. There we were, a class of twenty kids from all different backgrounds, painting together. The sun shining through the window felt like an omen of hope.

Moments of healing can often be found in the midst of hard times, especially if I seek them.

I AM OFTEN AWARE OF A PRESSURE TO LOOK GOOD.

The pressure to be beautiful is a very strange part of being a girl. I know we all care about our clothes and makeup and hair, but I know some girls who care about nothing else. That doesn't seem quite right, plus it can get boring.

I don't quite know what to do about this pressure, except to talk about it. I don't want it to have too much power in my life. The definition of beauty is key here. My mom says ideas of beauty are much broader in other cultures than in America. Maybe we could start to widen the definition by seeing all sorts of different people as beautiful, each in their own way.

Writing exercise: I will write about how our culture's definition of beauty has hurt me or my friends. Then I'll write about what I'd like a definition of beauty to include.

BEING A GOOD SPORT ISN'T ALWAYS EASY.

My little cousin who is only five has become a card shark. He hates to lose and usually makes a lot of complaining noises when he does. His mother keeps saying to him, "You have to learn to be a good sport about losing. No one can win every game."

When Andrea's research project took first place and mine took third, I wanted to whine, too. Instead, I put a smile on my face and congratulated Andrea. I could tell she really appreciated my response. I took my disappointment home to my mom, who understood and was proud of how gracious I was to Andrea.

No one can win all the time. It's important to learn how to lose gracefully, how to be happy for other's successes.

STEP TO THE MUSIC OF YOUR OWN DRUM.

Sometimes I float between different groups at school. There's the jock group and the intellectuals and the party-ers and more. In each group there are different pressures. In one group, if you use drugs or drink a lot, you're cool; in another group, if you're an athletic success, you're cool. In another group, you have to have read *War and Peace* to be cool.

There's power in the expectations and especially in the group pressure. That's why it's so important to know my own values and strengths and what's important to me. My older brother says I can talk to him anytime I'm struggling with this. I often do. My best friend Lizzie and I talk about it, too, especially when one of us is feeling pulled in a way that doesn't feel quite right.

I don't have to do anything that doesn't feel right or genuine to me in order to belong. I have a special place in this world, and I can just be me.

WHAT ABOUT DATING?

For so long my girlfriends and I just hung out and now some of us are starting to date. We do more with boys as a group, too, and this seems to change things. Sometimes we all act a bit different when boys are around.

Dating opened a whole new world for me and my friends. It's fun and exciting and a little nerve-wracking. It helps that I have a good friend who is male: my neighbor Jeremy, whom I've known since we went to kindergarten together. Even though having a crush is exciting, I like my friendship with him because we appreciate and respect each other–neither one of us has too much power.

*I want the balance of a healthy friendship
to be part of any dating I do.*

RESPONSIBLE USE OF MONEY IS SOMETHING I CAN LEARN.

My older brother has a tendency to spend money impulsively and then to be without it until he builds his supply back up. It's harder for me to spend. I tend to hoard money and am always trying to get my parents to spring for me so I can save what's mine.

My dad says that balance is important and that we learn through trial and error. I get an allowance and make babysitting money, and in the summer I teach swim lessons. Dad makes me save half of what I earn and put it in the bank for my college fund. The rest is mine to spend. It's not always easy deciding how and where to use my money best. My dad says many adults struggle with this, too. His rules are: don't spend what you don't have and be thoughtful about your spending and saving.

I need to think about money and learn to use it responsibly.

I WANT TO TAKE TIME TO APPRECIATE MY PARENTS.

One thing I've learned from my friend Julia, whose dad died, is how important it is to love and appreciate my parents. I don't know why this is so easy to forget, but it is. They do so much for me, but often I just take them for granted. But my friend is so sad to have her dad gone, and I know I would be, too.

I often think about how the rising sun, especially in the warmer months, wakes up the plants and animals. Birds begin to sing, plants open up, and leaves on trees turn green. When I thank my parents and let them know how much I appreciate them, they brighten up, sing a little (maybe), and we all feel warmer.

*Appreciating my parents is like letting
the sun shine from me onto our family.*

RESPECTING EACH OTHER IS PART OF FAMILY HEALTH.

For a while my older brother was making fun of me and my friends. He mimicked the way we talked to each other and made fun of our makeup. My friends and I felt bad.

My mom and dad stepped in and talked to him for a long time. Then we had a family meeting and talked about respecting each other, even if we didn't agree with each other's choices about friends, clothing, and activities. Name-calling is definitely out the window now. We're all still working on this, but I feel like my brother gives me and my friends a lot more respect and I'm working on giving the same respect to my little brother.

I know how bad it feels to not be treated with respect. Respect is a simple but very important gift we can give each other in our family.

MAY THE SUN SHINE WARM UPON YOUR FACE
AND THE WIND BE ALWAYS AT YOUR BACK.
–AN OLD IRISH BLESSING

Our neighbors always put up green lights and sham-
rocks for St. Patrick's Day, and sometimes they deliver
cookies shaped like four-leafed clovers. They make the
day seem especially festive. If it's warm enough for the
windows to be open, I can hear Irish harp music floating
out into the air. It is so beautiful and soothing.

I love that old Irish blessing. My favorite line is, May
the road rise to meet you. This sounds to me like, May
the path of your life open up in front of you. This idea
makes my heart happy.

*I think that whether I'm Irish or not, a bit of that green Irish
luck is in the air for me and all my friends today.*

WHEN YOU'RE FEELING DOWN, FIND A COUPLE OF WAYS TO COMFORT YOURSELF.

Some days I just wake up feeling a little down. I may be able to pinpoint what's weighing on me, but then again, I may not. It could be disappointment over a grade or over not being chosen by a friend or teacher for a special activity. There are times when there's tension in my family, and this can bring me down.

My favorite teacher, Mr. Hunter, says this is completely normal. He claims these feelings can be turned into creative energy. Paint it, he says, write a poem about it, play it on the piano or your saxophone. Or talk it over with a friend who understands. When I do any of these things, I feel comforted and the weight begins to lift.

Writing exercise: I will write about some of my favorite ways to comfort myself when I'm feeling down.

Express affection.

My friend Angie is so good at just telling people when they look great or when they've done something well. Compliments come out of her mouth so easily and naturally. I admire this in her. For one thing, it makes everybody around her feel good. For another, she frees the rest of us to be more expressive about what we like in each other.

Sometimes I think about withholding affection as having our arms crossed and held tight against us, whereas expressing affection is having our arms and hands open out toward each other and the world. It makes me think of the Beatles' song, "And in the end the love you take is equal to the love you make."

When I feel affection and admiration today, I will express it rather than keep it to myself. This expands the love in my life.

SPRING BEGINS TO SING.

The spring equinox marks the beginning of a season of hopefulness. After the quiet hibernation of winter when we go inside of ourselves more than usual, spring begins with a soft hum. It's quiet at first, inviting us out of our caves. Small green buds emerge, so slow and tiny at first. I know that weeks from now there will the fast-growing splashes of green, a feast for the senses.

But today I like to honor the quiet entrance of spring, the soft hum of its energy. I like to think about what parts of me are emerging, aspects I want to nurture in the warm sun rays and gentle winds to come.

!

Writing exercise: I will write about spring's arrival and what I want to see emerge in my life this spring.

REFLECTION IS A DEEP POOL.

Last winter I was sick for a couple of weeks. This forced me to do quiet things: I wrote in my journal a lot, read books, played the piano, drew with my colored pencils and markers. Part of me hated this enforced slowing down. Another part of me became strong and centered. When I went back to feeling well and being busy, I noticed it was easier to be peaceful: it was like I had built up my peaceful reserves.

When I regularly take quiet time, I feel less scattered and frenzied. I am more balanced and centered and this feels great. I don't want to be a shallow person and dipping into the pool of reflection deepens my life.

I will take time to do something quiet and reflective, especially when I'm feeling anxious or frustrated.

DOUBT AND FAITH GO TOGETHER.

The other day my friend and I had a long talk about God and the Great Spirit. She goes to church a lot and is involved in Sunday School classes. My family goes sometimes. Another friend of mine has a father who is Zen Buddhist, and they have regular quiet/meditation time at their house. Another friend goes on retreats in the woods.

Aunt Jane says there are many ways to honor the quiet spirit alive in us and in every other living thing. Together, we create a weaving of many colors and textures. What's important is to take the time to reflect and honor our spiritual lives.

Even in the midst of busy days, it helps to reflect on the spiritual part of our lives.

EMBRACE DEATH AS YOU WILL LIFE,
FOR THEY ARE ONE AND THE SAME.
–Kahlil Gibran

A good friend of mine, Creona, has a brother who was in a serious car accident. He's been in the hospital for a month and gets to come home soon, but he may be paralyzed from the waist down. My friends and I have helped baby-sit Creona's little sister because her parents need to be at the hospital so much. Our families have all brought food over and done what we could to help.

It's hard to understand why such a sad thing happens, but at the same time, there was such incredible love and concern for this family. Creona's mom said the support that came to their family renewed her faith in the goodness of people. This goodness touches us all.

Writing exercise: I will list all the people I know who would help me and my family if we needed it. Then I'll create an image that conveys this love.

HONOR THE DAILY WORK OF DREAMS.

Last year I heard the song "Memory" from Cats and decided I wanted to learn it on the piano. My piano teacher said it would be a good challenge for me. I practiced it and all my other lessons almost every day. I took one day off a week, but otherwise, I played every day.

At first the song was like a foreign language. All those notes, all over the scale. I spent weeks deciphering each measure, first the upper clef, then the lower clef. And at first I played it slowly and unevenly. But a year later, I play it smoothly and have passages memorized. Knowing this piece of music feels wonderful: it was worth all the practice.

Dreams, big and small, are worth pursuing. The daily work is enriching, and the end result feels great!

IT'S OKAY TO ASK QUESTIONS.

Sometimes there are things going on that I don't quite get, like there's a fog hanging in the air. Maybe it's a math problem I don't understand, and the fog lies between me and the solution. Another time I may notice a friend pulling back from me, and I don't understand why. Or my mom may have a bad day, and that doesn't make sense to me.

When the fog settles in, it's time to ask questions. I asked for special help from my math teacher: she was there to teach. I asked my friend what was going on: there was something I had said that bothered her and there was something going on at home she needed to talk about. I asked my mom, in as caring a tone as I could, if she was having a bad day. She appreciated my caring enough to ask.

Questions can help lift the fog. They are always okay to ask.

CAST OFF THE SHADOW OF SHAME.

Have you ever walked away from a conversation with someone and realized you're walking away feeling bad? Something was said, maybe directly, but more often indirectly, that entered you and made you feel put down, diminished, or shamed.

This can come from anyone: teacher, friend, parent, the parent of a friend. But when it happens, it's important to sift through and reflect on what happened. Question it. Do I need to talk more with this person to clarify what he or she said and how I feel about it? Is there something I need to learn from what's been said? Or do I need to let it go and realize that sometimes other people's bad days can cast a shadow across mine?

It's possible to shake off the shadow of a sour conversation by questioning it, doing what I need to do, and then letting the shadow go. It doesn't always belong to me.

FOLLOW YOUR HEART, LOVE WILL FIND YOU,
TRUTH WILL UNBIND YOU,
SING OUT A SONG OF THE SOUL.
–CRIS WILLIAMSON

My heart sings when I'm singing. It sings when I'm laughing with a friend or really listening to her. It sings when I'm doing well in school. It sings when I'm flying down a ski hill on a sunny winter day. It sings when I'm helping other people.

I like to be around people who help my heart to sing, who encourage and get behind my passions. I love the idea that if I pursue my passions and interests, love will come find me, and the truth of my love will free me. Free me to sing the song of my soul every day.

*Writing exercise: Over a period of a couple of days,
I will write in detail about all the things
that make my heart sing. What does it mean to me,
right now in my life, to follow my heart?*

COOL AS A POOL IN THE JUNGLE OF NOOL.
–DR. SEUSS

I keep noticing different ways people try to be cool. There's a guy in my science class who thinks he's cool because he keeps talking back to the teacher and then mimicking him. Sometimes we can't help but laugh, but most of us think he's pretty negative and mean.

I see some kids using drugs, skipping school, or getting involved in gangs to be cool. But these are short-lived kinds of cool: I've seen this in my cousin. Drugs took over his life, and now he's a college dropout, while many of his friends have jobs that they love and interests that they're pursuing. Their lives look a lot more cool than his.

I

Long-term, genuine coolness is constructive, not destructive.

WE ARE ALL PART OF A GREATER WHOLE.

My humanities teacher this year is so good at having us think about ourselves as a part of a larger community. We get credits for doing "service work": working with older people or the mentally ill, tutoring low-income children. I tutored a third-grade girl at my neighborhood elementary school. She was having a hard time with her reading and wasn't getting much help at home. I helped her once a week and could see a slow improvement. She and I really liked each other.

This experience broke open my view of the world, like looking at the land from the window of an airplane or a high place. It's a big world, and there are many struggling people. Stepping out of the comfort of my life stretches me, helps me remember I'm a small, but important part of a big world.

Anything I can do to reach out does make a difference.

GRATITUDE MEANS BEING GENEROUS
WITH YOUR THANKS.

This week my teacher thanked me for all the good questions I bring to class and my mom thanked me for helping out with my younger brother when she was sick. It felt great to be thanked, to know that I'm appreciated.

I realize I need to do more of this kind of thanking, too. I saw my dad's face light up when I thanked him for the great spaghetti dinner he fed me and my friends. And the last time Mom gave me a ride, I made a big deal out of thanking her. She broke into a big smile.

Thanking those who do things for me is
like brushing sunshine across the day.

TALKING OFTEN RELEASES THE PRESSURE.

It's amazing to me how little things that bother me can add up. My mother has been crabby all week, I'm worried about my research paper that's due soon, and my friend Jenny is depressed because her boyfriend broke up with her. But I've been so busy I haven't had time to talk or think much about these things. Just the same, they have been weighing me down.

Until last night. I had a long conversation on the phone with my good friend Angie. We are both worried about Jenny, and it helped to share our worry. After I talked to Angie, I had a long talk with my dad, too. He helped me set up a schedule for my research paper and said he'd talk to Mom. None of my problems disappeared, but talking about them made me feel less overwhelmed and less weighted down.

Talking with a trusted person always eases my burdens.

APRIL

LIFE IS AN ADVENTURE.

I have a crazy uncle I just love. He flies a small airplane all over the country for his job, especially over wilderness. At different times, he has skis, pontoons, or wheels on his plane, so he can land anywhere, anytime. His whole approach to life is full of zest and possibility.

I admire this in him and I feel that kind of energy when I approach my life in the same way. I have adventures all the time: flying down a ski trail, trying out for the school play, practicing a new skill. Even getting to know a new friend or writing a poem is adventurous. These things carry me into new terrain.

Writing exercise: I will write two pages of healthy adventures I want to explore in my life.

VARIETY IS THE SPICE OF LIFE.

Looking at a garden full of flowers, I enjoy all the different colors and shapes and notice how they complement one another. One blooms at a different time than others, one sends out its scent at night while another shines its brightest in the midday sun. We don't feel the need to put one flower down in favor of another.

What makes it so easy to put myself or others down? Comparisons arise from a narrow vision, and in the words of that famous Grinch, they shrink my heart. When I compare myself with others and use the comparison to make myself feel bad or superior, I need to open my eyes and my heart. If it's Ellie's turn to shine today, I can celebrate with her, just like I want her to celebrate with me when it's my turn.

In the garden of friendship, I can enjoy and honor each of my friend's strengths and shining times, as well as honor my own.

I NEED TO TAKE TIME TO NURTURE
MY FAMILY RELATIONSHIPS.

Nine times out of ten, I'd rather be with my friends than my family. I hate to miss out on anything. But I also need the foundation of my family. They're a solid rock I can fly away from, but I always depend on them being there when I return. I've noticed that when I'm most sure of that rock, I have the greatest strength for flying.

One of the ways I strengthen that sense of a foundation is by taking time to be with my family. Sometimes this means a simple, leisurely meal, when I don't take phone calls from friends. Shopping trips with my mom are always a special time for us. When my dad takes just me skiing or to the movies, I feel special. One night my brothers and I weren't feeling well, and we all played cards. It was fun and felt really comforting.

*Even though I usually want to be with my friends,
I know I depend on the rock foundation of my family.*

I NEED TO ACCEPT MYSELF.

It's so easy to tell myself what's wrong with me: I'm not quite thin enough; I should have gotten an A, not a B, on my essay; I wish I had scored the winning goal in the soccer tournament last week. I was so tired last night that I broke down and cried when my mom came in to say good night. I started to tell her all these things and she held me and told me all my strengths and how much she loved me.

It was like the world shifted: I felt the tension drain out of my body. Warmth replaced the coldness. Suddenly I was able to see all the things in my life I felt good about. A peacefulness, like standing beneath a beautiful waterfall, surrounded me.

Writing exercise: When I'm being hard on myself,
I need to shift my focus. I'll write a list of all the things
I am and do that I really love. If I need help with this,
I can always ask someone who loves me.

No two people can live together
without occasional conflict.

I hate it when my parents argue. My mom says part
of loving is occasionally disagreeing. She says that what
is not okay is calling each other names or doing the
cold, silent treatment instead of talking. Listening to
each other, she says, is important.

My favorite times are when my mom and dad end an
argument by laughing about how they drive each other
crazy. My dad is good at bringing humor into hard
moments. He does it with me, too. Maybe what I can
learn from watching them is how to disagree with people I love. I can do this by talking about my feelings. I
can resist the urge to name-call, especially with my
brother. If I don't get started, I am more able to listen to
him.

*Trading different points of view is part of being in a
relationship. I need to be willing to talk about my
feelings and to listen to the other person's, too.*

KEEP THE FAITH, BABY.

Faith means different things to different people. My grandmother is very religious, and she says her faith gets her up in the morning and through everything. My aunt is not very religious, but she says you have to have faith in life—the goodness of life—and in yourself. The opposite of faith, she believes, is fear or hopelessness.

A boy in the senior class committed suicide. Suicide must be the ultimate form of not having faith. The counselors said he could have gotten professional help, that there are often chemical reasons for feeling so bleak about life. Lately I've been thinking about faith as a way of believing in the goodness of life, in spite of life's imperfections. Faith is like the spring that feeds the lake. It keeps bubbling up, keeping the water clean, refreshed, and nourished.

When fear or hopelessness rises in me, I can dip into the spring-fed depths of my own faith in life. If I need help to do this, there are people around who can help me.

FEELINGS REQUIRE EXPRESSION, NOT REPRESSION.

We have one bush in our yard that an insect burrowed inside of, and the stem grew around this insect, making the bush look misshapen. My mom says that's what happens to feelings that we don't acknowledge, that we keep hidden. Hidden feelings tend to misshape us.

I was mad at my mom because she argued with my dad the night before last. When I came home from school, I was mean to her, even though she was letting me have a friend over for dinner. She pulled me aside and said, "What's the deal? Here I'm letting you have Ellie over, and you're treating me like dirt. I don't get it." Out came my feelings about the other night. We had a good talk and she reassured me about her love for dad and their need for an occasional argument. It felt good to have my feelings out in the open instead of burrowing under my skin, affecting my behavior.

Feelings need the light of open air and sunshine.
I can let them out by talking, reflecting, expressing
my feelings in writing, music, or exercise.

BUDDHA TAUGHT PEOPLE TO LIVE GOOD LIVES.
–FAITH WINCHESTER

In Asian cultures, many people worship Buddha. He was born a prince in India in 563 B.C.E., but he left a life of luxury and money to meditate. He wanted to take away all human suffering. After he died, his followers started Buddhism.

On this day, his birthday, people polish his shrines and statues and people visit them with flowers. In fact, in Japan the day is called Hana Matsuri, or Festival of the Flowers. This day has been celebrated for over 1,300 years. What is admired about Buddha is his focus on the life of the spirit and the way he turned away from money and possessions. Flowers are a wonderful way to celebrate and honor the life of the spirit.

Writing exercise: I will think and then write about what most religions have in common. How are my religious or spiritual beliefs similar to those of people all over the world?

Consider me
...
Black
Caught in a crack
...
Consider me,
Descended also
From the
Mystery.
–Langston Hughes

On this day in 1866, the Civil Rights Act was passed, making black Americans U.S. citizens. My friend Shaiwan says its still painful to think of her ancestors as slaves, working so hard and having so few rights. She still feels sadness and sometimes anger. Last week her brother was arrested and held for questioning for a short time. It turned out to be a case of mistaken identity. Still, he felt like it was his blackness that made him suspicious, not anything he had done or was doing.

There are still inequities in our world. I feel like I need to be considerate and aware of these inequities and yet remember that we're all descended from and part of the same mystery. Of life.

On this day, I honor the civil rights
of all people on our planet.

PASSOVER, WHICH COMES EVERY SPRING,
IS EVERY JEWISH CHILD'S FAVORITE HOLIDAY.
–RUTH BRIN

Although the date that Passover begins is different every year because of the lunar calendar, it always comes in March or April, and it's celebrated for eight days. The seder or passover dinner (which is what Jesus' Last Supper was) uses food for celebration and symbolism.

Eggs represent springtime. Bitter herbs represent the bitter taste of slavery. Matzo (unleavened bread) and lamb are also important and ceremonial parts of the meal. I recently went to my first seder at my friend Rebecca's house, and it was a feast for the senses. The smells of the food and the ceremonial oil and the strong, sharp tastes of the food, and then the sound of singing and prayers in Hebrew! Many of the songs sung were about having faith in final redemption by God.

*If I ever feel like I'm surviving a bad time,
I can remember the rich and difficult history of the Jews
and the beautiful rituals they created to commemorate
their survival against great odds.*

MY CHILDHOOD MEMORIES OF
CHURCH SERVICES AROUND EASTER ARE FILLED
WITH MYSTERY, LONGING, AND THEN HOPE.

Sometime in late March or April. Christians all over the world honor the death and resurrection of Christ. The Good Friday service at my church always makes me cry. There's something about the songs, the images of Mary watching her son suffer on the cross, and Jesus feeling abandoned by God, his father, that all work together on my heart. The church is dark when we leave, all lights out except for candles. I walk out, feeling hushed and electrically alive.

Then, two days later, the church is filled with white Easter lilies and the music is celebratory and we sing alleluia for the first time since Lent began weeks earlier. It's so hopeful and joyous. The passage from death to rebirth or resurrection is a theme in many myths and legends and all major religions. I think we humans desperately need reminders that our wounds can heal, that dead parts of us can be reborn.

Let me enter fully into the sadness and longing that prepare
me for the miracle of rebirth and resurrection.

DO YOU KNOW ADULTS AND KIDS WHO ARE SO SERIOUS
THEY DON'T REALLY KNOW HOW TO HAVE FUN?

Being able to have fun is an important part of life. Of course, it's important to not make it the only important thing, to the point where you neglect responsibilities. Genuine fun includes laughter, having a sense of humor, being able to enjoy other people, and doing things that are lighthearted and feel good.

My Aunt Jane says that having lots of healthy ways to have fun can keep us from getting into trouble. I have a lot of fun with my friends; playing in the jazz band is a gas, and I'm crazy about skiing and soccer. What I notice about fun is that it energizes me.

*Writing exercise: I'll make a list of all the ways
I have fun and enjoy my world. Then I'll choose
one or two items from my list to do today.*

A NECESSARY INGREDIENT FOR HAPPINESS
IS NOT HAVING EVERYTHING WE WANT.
—BERTRAND RUSSELL

This quote is prominently displayed on my favorite aunt's refrigerator. It rings a bell inside me. My parents tell me all the time that I have to shift my focus from what I want to appreciating what I have. I can't help but want some of the things my friends have or that I see advertised. But when I stay focused on them, I feel anxious, frustrated. There's an uneasiness that comes with wanting too much, because I always want more.

When I listen to that bell ringing inside me, I notice my healthy body, my family members who care about me, good friends, music lessions, and sports activities. There's always food on the table. When I slow down and appreciate what I have, I find that gratefulness moves through me like warm sunshine, energizing and calming me.

Writing exercise: I'll write about all the things in my life I am grateful for. First, make a list, then write about one or two items on my list in great detail (including smells, colors, a specific meal, or lessons).

HELPING OUT IS PART OF FAMILY LIFE.

"Cleaning day," my dad will say. Or he'll tell me it's my night to do dishes. Grrr . . . I want to say. "No. I have better things to do." He'll say, "I know the feeling, but we don't want to live in a garbage house, do we?"

Chores around the house are just a part of life. My dad is always saying, "Many hands make light work." Rather than fighting him, lately I've been trying to find ways to make it more fun. Sometimes I put on my favorite CD and rock out as I clean. It's easier to do chores than to think about them. Doing dishes or dusting can be relaxing and peaceful when I get in the right frame of mind.

*The responsibilities I have as part of my family
are things I will always have to do—I may as well
learn to do them with some joy.*

A GESTURE OF KINDNESS IS A
SIMPLE GIFT AND GOOD GIFT.

Kindness is a quality I admire in others, especially in my friends. I'm often kind to my friends. It's harder to be kind at home, to my younger brother and older brother and parents. Any bad feelings I have tend to come out at home in the form of meanness.

Yet when I make a gesture of kindness, it feels like fresh air blowing into a stale room. I complimented my younger brother on the artwork he brought home and suddenly he would do anything I asked of him. I told my mom she looked really pretty, and she wasn't crabby anymore. I asked my dad how his day at work went, and then I listened. He seemed surprised but happy to talk. I actually felt better about myself. I wonder why choosing to be kind rather than mean to people I love seems so hard?

I will make a conscious effort to be a force of kindness in my family.

LINGERING SUN: RIVERS AND MOUNTAINS BRIGHTEN.
SPRING WINDS: FLOWERS AND GRASS GIVE OUT SCENT.
–Tu Fu (712 - 770 C.E.)

I woke up this morning to an open window and cur-
tains blowing gently in the breeze. Into my room came
the smells of the neighbor's lilacs and the grass my dad
mowed the night before. Then I remembered biking
around the lake last night and being amazed by the row
of cherry and apple trees in bloom and fragrant. I
breathed deep while stretching out in my bed.

This time of year is so fragrant. Smells come to me
and seem to carry armfuls of kindness and sweetness
and gentleness. No matter what my worries of the day
are, fragrant smells enter me and I'm happy.

*This time of year is so special that it's important
to take a little time every day to notice what's blooming
and to breathe nature's amazing scents.*

I BEGAN TO SEE THAT HOPE, HOWEVER FEEBLE ITS
APPARENT FOUNDATION, BESPEAKS ALLEGIANCE TO EVERY
UNLIKELY BEAUTY THAT REMAINS INTACT ON EARTH.
–DAVID JAMES DUNCAN

When I heard the news about my cousin ending up
in the hospital from an overdose of drugs, I went to my
favorite spot by the lake near my house. I listened to the
lapping water, let its deep blue enter and soothe me. A
great blue heron perched nearby and when it lifted its
wings and slid gracefully from the top of the trees into
the sky, I felt my heavy heart lift a bit.

Life is good, that beautiful bird seemed to say to me,
even though it is full of heartbreak. Difficult times,
either in my personal life or in the world, sometimes
bring doubt or despair. Often it is the world's beauty
that stirs hope in me again.

*Writing exercise: I will describe in detail one
beautiful thing I have noticed in the natural world
recently and explore what it tells me about life.*

FRIENDSHIPS MAKE THE WORLD A WARMER PLACE.

My good friend Lizzie recently had a serious form of pneumonia. She was in the hospital for ten days, and for a few of those days everyone was afraid she might die. She's okay now and back home, but the whole experience brought our group of friends closer. We all realized how much we didn't want to lose Lizzie: how much she means to all of us. This also made us realize how much we mean to each other. When she was too sick for visitors, we called her mother every day to see how Lizzie was doing. And when she was better, we visited, a couple of us at a time, so we wouldn't wear her out. She was so happy to see us!

Now we're collecting homework for her. And I can see how much her parents appreciate the way we cheer her up.

In sad and difficult times, it's the love of friends and family that brings comfort.

GOALS—YOU GO, GIRL!

On the first day of ninth grade, our humanities teacher had us write out goals. Mine were to make two new friends, be on the honor roll, make the soccer team, and not go down a bad road (taking drugs) like my cousin did. When he got into drugs, he didn't care much anymore about his goals. He still wanted to do well in school, but he cared more about getting high.

I've got my list of goals up on my bulletin board in my room. My mom and dad say they're proud of my goals, and that feels good, too. I love that saying from the Olympics, "Go for the Gold." So at the top of the page, I've written Go for the Goal.

Writing exercise: I'll make a list of my goals, title and color it, and put it up where I can see it easily.

NOT MUCH HAPPENS WITHOUT DISCIPLINE.

Daily discipline is the part of life that often feels ho-hum, but without which nothing happens. I moan and groan about having to practice my saxophone or my piano, but I know it's that half hour of practice (almost) every day that makes me play better and better.

It's the same with homework. So much of my life right now is about learning and creating habits of learning. What I learn now will help carry me through the rest of my life. A lot of the time, even when I initially don't feel like practicing or doing my math, I get into it, I enjoy it. The payoff for daily discipline—with homework, music, anything artistic or athletic—is huge: deep and steady growth in my skills.

Daily discipline,
although not always easy,
is often enjoyable.

HONOR MY BODY.

I've always heard the expression that the body is the temple of the spirit. My mom is a health nut, and she is always telling me how important it is to eat healthy food and to exercise. I see some people smoking already and experimenting with drugs and alcohol. The other thing my mother says is that I'm too young, emotionally and physically, to be experimenting. She says it slows you down and clouds you up.

I don't always want to listen to my mother, but I can see what she means. The people I most admire in school and out in the world are those ones who care about their dreams and their bodies. Maybe those go hand in hand. If I want to be a great soccer player, I eat well and work out a lot. If I want to be a great writer, I take care of my health so I can get up every morning and write. It is through my body that I am able to accomplish or experience anything.

Writing exercise: I'll list all the things
my body does for me and then all the ways
I can take care of it, honor it, and keep it healthy.

I LOVE THE EARTH WITH ALL OF MYSELF BECAUSE IT IS
THE HAVEN OF HUMANITY, THE MANIFEST SPIRIT OF GOD.
–KAHLIL GIBRAN

Today is Earth Day, a day to think about and pay attention to how we live on our earth. A day to celebrate loving this earth. My mom said when she was in high school, her class got on a bus and went to a bare hillside and planted trees all day to celebrate Earth Day. When she goes back to her hometown now, the pine trees they planted fill the hillside with their deep greenery.

Planting is a way to celebrate the earth. So is gathering rocks or just taking a walk and smelling the emerging flowers and green leaves and grass. Loving the wind on my face. The warmth of the sun soaking into me. Loving the feel and mood of a light rain or a white snowfall.

The earth is my haven, my home, and my best
answer to the question: Is there a God?

FOLLOW YOUR DREAMS.

My friend Angie dreams of becoming a concert pianist. Julia's dream is playing soccer well enough to get a college scholarship. Shaiwan's dream is to be a professional dancer. Being a track star is important to me, and I also like to write poems in my journal. One day Lee wants to go to China, where she was born.

Sometimes dreams are small and sometimes they are big. Lately I've been thinking of dreams as the rich soil that makes our gardens grow. My English teacher had us write about our dreams, and it was fascinating to hear the variety of dreams my classmates have. Our teacher said the saddest people are the ones who have given up their dreams for lack of hope or encouragement. It's so important to encourage each other's and our own dreams–to keep fertilizing the ground so that beautiful flowers can blossom.

Writing exercise: I'll make a list of my dreams, small and big ones, and post them in my journal or on my bedroom wall so they can fertilize my daily life.

THE WORLD'S BEAUTY IS ALWAYS THERE.

Sometimes I am so focused on my own life that I don't pay attention to the world around me. I walk around with my head down. But we've been reading Thoreau's Walden in English, and it's got me paying attention to what's around me more. This morning I sat at my bedroom window and watched the sun break over the oak trees in my neighbor's yard. The swirls of rose and yellow in the clouds made me feel happy and grateful to be here.

The purple tulips my mom and I planted when I was six are still coming up, year after year. When I stop to think about it, this is amazing. Every day the trees and sky look a little different; every day presents its own unique beauty. When I let this beauty in, I feel grateful to be alive and here.

Nature's beauty is one of life's great gifts:
it requires no fee, only my attentiveness.

BE MYSELF.

Sounds simple, doesn't it? Actually, it is simple. But it's tricky too, because I'm still trying to figure out who I am, still trying out different ways of being. Sometimes I find myself admiring and trying to be like the most boisterous and outgoing students at school. Other times I find myself admiring and wanting to be more like the quiet, kind, gentle ones. I'll hear myself borrowing a phrase or a gesture from someone else, or even from a movie.

I guess I'm still impressionable. Aunt Jane says that it's okay to try on different aspects of my personality, that being myself doesn't mean I stay the same all the time; it includes changes. She says the key is to pay attention to how I feel inside more than to how people react to me. When my behavior matches how I feel inside in a good way, then I am being myself.

*Being myself means knowing how I really
feel inside and being able to express that.*

ALL SANITY DEPENDS ON THIS:
THAT IT SHOULD BE A DELIGHT TO FEEL HEAT STRIKE
THE SKIN, A DELIGHT TO STAND UPRIGHT, KNOWING
THE BONES ARE MOVING EASILY UNDER THE FLESH.
–DORIS LESSING

Last year I had a broken leg. It was a major pain to go anywhere. Whenever I think about that time, I appreciate my ability to walk, run, climb stairs, throw my legs over the side of the bed and get up easily every morning.

Every spring I love the feel of the sun on my skin. I'm careful to not get sunburned and I wear sun protection, but I also love what I think of as the caressing fingers of the spring sun. It's like the sun's rays reach inside me and warm and massage my winter-tight bones.

*Life is good and sane when I can appreciate walking
and soaking up nature's treats, especially the sun.*

I LISTEN TO THE WIND, TO THE WIND OF MY SOUL.
–Cat Stevens

Last night the wind blew fiercely all night long. The willow tree outside my bedroom swayed its branches back and forth, brushing my window. The sounds seemed to move in and out of my dreams, and I could feel them cleansing me in an unexpected way.

Sometimes I get so caught up in small worries like homework, who is more popular than I am, is my friend Jenny mad at me or just busy. Listening to the wind felt like the universe was knocking at my door. That wind blew my worries away and made me excited to be alive and part of a world that includes trees and wind.

When I feel a part of something large and important, then I feel grateful. And when I feel grateful, I feel more at peace. I will listen to the wind and see what it has to teach me about my world and myself.

LIFE WOULD HAVE BEEN SO MUCH EASIER
IF SOMEONE HAD SAT ME DOWN AND TOLD ME
THE REAL RULES: THAT THE GUY YOU THOUGHT WAS
'ALL THAT' WHEN YOU WERE 13 WOULD MAKE
YOU GAG WHEN YOU WERE THIRTY.
–COURTNEY COX ARQUETTE

I guess it's helpful to know that life changes. I will change. The people around me will change. Even though Brian is Mr. Popular and ignores me and I can't seem to care about any other boy in our class, this too will change. I can't wait for that change. Maybe it's beginning just a bit. I can think of some things about Brian that irritate me, and Creona has always thought he was a jerk.

There's this guy in my speech class who in spite of always having been kind of quiet is really funny. He's self-assured in a gentle way and as we work on our class project together, he's becoming a friend.

My attraction to people seems to be changing. I want to go with these changes and not hang onto the past.

QUESTION AUTHORITY, BUT DON'T BE A JERK.
SOME RULES ARE STUPID, BUT SOME ACTUALLY
ARE THERE FOR A REASON. LEARN THE DIFFERENCE.
–MINDY MORGENSTERN

Sometimes I just feel rebellious, especially toward my mom. I fight her rules. I used to fight the seat-belt rule when I was in the back seat and sneak by without doing the buckle, just to feel like I was pulling a fast one on her. When I look back at this now, I think it was so stupid.

Last month some kids in our school were in a car accident, and the ones who were not buckled in were seriously hurt. It will be months before they can walk normally again. Pretty huge price to pay for a little rebellion.

*I hope I learn to use common sense and maturity
about which rules to question and which to follow.*

BEING ALONE IS GOOD FOR MY SOUL.

This morning I woke early to finish an art project that's due this week. I sat on my bed with colored pencils and watercolors all around me. I was supposed to draw water, and I worked from a photograph my dad had taken of me standing in a waterfall. I loved looking at that picture and trying to get the right shade of blue for the spray of the waterfall.

Time flew by. And even though I hadn't wanted to work on this project, I loved doing it. Just being by myself and working with that picture and all those beautiful colors made me feel peaceful inside. Then I knew what my mom meant when she said it's important to be able to be alone and enjoy it. Besides making me feel peaceful, the experience also made me feel strong. For that period of time, I needed nothing else in order to feel content.

I will remember that being alone
can help center, heal, and energize me.

MAY

I WOULD BE A FOX, OR A TREE
FULL OF WAVING BRANCHES.
–MARY OLIVER

In writing class we had an assignment to write about what we would be if we were a plant, tree, flower, or animal. It was fascinating what we came up with, and most of us read our exercises out loud. Maria wanted to be a fox so she could be more sharp-eyed. Yolanda wanted to be one of the birds that sing in the tree outside her window each morning, waking the world with songs of joy.

Tom, who is usually so tough, wanted to be an oak leaf, soaking up sun, blowing in the breezes, turning colors slowly and beautifully. I wanted to be one of the crocuses in my front yard, the first one to announce the new and hopeful season of spring, the brilliant purple shining against new green.

Writing exercise: I will write about what I would be
as a different part of nature. What might I feel, see,
look like, and notice about our amazing world?

SURVIVAL IS A MATTER OF THE SPIRIT.

Today, May 2, is Holocaust Remembrance Day. When my family went to Washington, D.C., we went through the Holocaust Museum. It was a sobering and impressive day for me. I learned so much, and often I felt tears in my eyes, especially for the Jewish children and teenagers who lived (and died) during World War II.

Reading and seeing a play about Anne Frank also affected me. I think about what courage it took to keep believing in the good things in life, even though she was in hiding, living in cramped and undesirable quarters, and always in danger. I think her writing must have helped her survive. More than anything, I admire her spirit: her open heart while living in closed conditions.

On this remembrance day, I want to remember and light a candle for those who suffered and died, and I want to honor and emulate the spiritual strength of survivors.

THE STORIES PEOPLE TELL HAVE A WAY OF
TAKING CARE OF THEM . . . THAT IS WHY WE
PUT THESE STORIES IN EACH OTHER'S MEMORY.
THIS IS HOW PEOPLE CARE FOR THEMSELVES.
—BARRY LOPEZ

My favorite kind of evening is spent talking with friends. We talk about our families and our dreams and our goals. We tell stories about what we did when we were younger. We swap stories about when we were the most scared or most nervous or most embarrassed.

I love stories. I love to tell them, and I love to hear them. They seem to me the best way of getting to know each other. Every story is its own—no two are alike. Years later I'll remember a story a friend told me, and it will make me laugh or comfort me, long after I've last heard it.

Stories live on in the listener's memory. Listening and telling stories are important gifts of friendship.

TALKING WITH ONE ANOTHER IS LOVING ONE ANOTHER.
–IVORY COAST

Occasionally my mom or dad takes me out for breakfast or dinner alone. This is great because we get a chance to talk, just the two of us. Sometimes I get so wrapped up in my life that I forget about talking to them. Or I'm upset with them and don't feel like talking.

But it really does help every time we talk, whether at a restaurant or our kitchen table or in the car. Even though I get mad at them, they are pretty reasonable human beings and are usually decent when it comes to listening to me. I just have to remember to talk, not to keep my thoughts bottled inside.

Talking is an important part of loving the people in my life.

SOMETIMES I IMAGINE THE PEOPLE WHO HAVE GONE
BEFORE US CHEERING US ON FROM THE OTHER SIDE.

In my Spanish class we made *ofrendes*, or offerings,
to people who have died. Then we had a celebration
called the Day of the Dead. This is a Mexican holiday
that celebrates the dead and honors their spirits, which
still live inside us.

I made an ofrende in honor of my Aunt Teresa, Dad's
sister, who I knew only a little bit before she died of cancer. She was a talented painter, and everybody says my
paintings remind them of hers. I sometimes feel that she
is around me in spirit, encouraging me to keep painting,
to believe in and keep developing my talent. I have a
small painting of hers, and it hangs beside my bed. I
often feel like I get strength from this painting, from my
memory of her.

One of the sources of strength in my life may
be from people who have gone before me.

SPENDING QUIET TIME ALONE GIVES YOUR MIND AN
OPPORTUNITY TO RENEW ITSELF AND CREATE ORDER.
–SUSAN TAYLOR

Lindsay and I are both messy. Yolanda and Jessica keep their rooms, folders, and backpacks neat as pins. Being organized and neat doesn't come very naturally to me at all. But I have noticed that when I slow down, it helps enormously. An evening in my room and, voila!, my room is picked up and I've organized all my school materials.

Being alone and quiet helps me in other ways, too. I take time to write letters to people I care about or to put up a poster I've been wanting to put up for weeks. I listen to my favorite new song until I've memorized the words. All of this helps me feel more peaceful and centered.

*Writing exercise: I will write a letter to a friend
or relative I haven't seen in a long time.*

THE TEENAGE GIRLS AND WOMEN WHO ARE
EXPERIENCING THE WORST PSYCHOLOGICAL VIOLENCE
ARE THE ONES LIVING ON LOWER INCOME.
–BYLLYE AVERY

A girl in my class wrote an amazing paper about how frightened she is of her mother's ex-husband. In the story, I could see how much lack of money affected everything. Her mother had to work two jobs. This girl, Sharina, was in charge of her two younger siblings a lot, and this guy would sometimes bring toys and money they couldn't get any other way. Still, he always became mean or hit them after he gave his gifts, so she and her mother weren't willing to see him anymore. But it wasn't easy.

I've always been friendly to Sharina which is why, I think, she showed me her paper. She also gave it to our teacher. She taught me a lot by letting me read how poverty affects people. Her and her mother's courage and hope in the face of difficult challenges also taught me a lot.

I hope I'll always be aware of people around me who have especially difficult lives. Let me be a force for kindness.

ONE DAY YOU FINALLY KNEW
WHAT YOU HAD TO DO, AND BEGAN . . .
–MARY OLIVER

I woke up the other day knowing I needed to apologize to my mother and little brother. My mother had said no to taking me shopping the night before, so I yelled and slammed doors and then made mean comments to her and my brother all evening. She kept sending me to my room, but I know the evening was really unpleasant for everybody.

She kept saying she would do nothing for me until I had mended what I had torn apart with my behavior. I sometimes think that life with loved ones contains a certain amount of tearing and repairing. My moods can be so strong and my emotions so on the surface that I sometimes do things I really regret later.

When I have torn a piece of the love between me and my family, it's important to find a way for me to mend it.

THE GRASS
LAY SOGGY AND LUSH IT WAS
LITTERED WITH PETALS ROUND THE CRABAPPLE TREE.
–DESMOND EGAN

Springtime is new life time. Green sprouts slowly at first, everywhere I look. I call this feather-green time, for the green is soft and delicate. Then suddenly, it seems, full leaves are out on all the trees, the grass has filled in on every hillside in every park. And the lilac trees! When I breathe deep around them or any other blossoming tree, there is such a gentle sweetness to the smell.

Springtime is full of sensual treats: colors and scents in particular. When I awake in the morning, all I have to do is look out my window. On my way to the bus stop, all I need to do is pay attention. There's a feast going on all round me. A feast of hope, color and beauty.

All I need to do is breathe deep and open my eyes to be energized by the miracle of spring.

MOTHER'S DAY IS A DAY TO HONOR MY MOTHER.

Mother's Day is just around the corner. Although I often struggle with my mother, I realize how much she does for me. And I don't often express that; it's a thought that mostly flashes by. For Mother's Day I'd like to collect all those flashes and do something nice for my mom.

My brothers and I are planning to serve her coffee and rolls in bed and to help with dishes all day long. We're going to make her a big card from the three of us. Since we have often forgotten to do anything, I know she will be touched and happy. I'm looking forward to it!

Writing exercise: I will write a list of all the things my mom does for me and then write her a special thank-you. She deserves a day of appreciation.

NEVER BEND YOUR HEAD. ALWAYS HOLD IT HIGH.
LOOK THE WORLD STRAIGHT IN THE EYE.
–HELEN KELLER

Sometimes I see people who seem a little afraid of life. This makes me feel sad for them. If I were them, I'd do everything I could to find out why I was afraid and try to change my feelings and approach to life.

I like the idea of this woman who was deaf and blind being so strong and proud. It helps me to remember that even on days when I struggle with my weaknesses or my mistakes, I can hold my head high and carry on. Courage is the word for this kind of attitude and for a certain love for life.

I can let my courage and love of life
outshine any regrets I have today.

EVERYBODY HAS GOT SOME GOOD.
SOME HIDE IT, SOME NEGLECT IT, BUT IT IS THERE.
–MOTHER TERESA

I have a tendency to be hard on people. I make judg-ments, close the door, and don't easily open it to some people. There's a boy in my class I shut out. He bugged me and seemed like a know-it-all. I figured if I never got to know him, that would be all right with me.

Then the school literary journal came out. He had a poem in there that was so beautiful and so sensitive. Then he played a solo on his saxophone in the jazz band, and suddenly he seemed pretty cool to me.

I need to remember that everybody has some good in them,
maybe far more goodness than I can readily see.

IT IS JUST LIKE THE HANDS
TO TELL THEIR STORIES WITHOUT SHAME.
EVEN HELD DOWN, THE WHITE KNUCKLEBONES
ASSERT THEMSELVES THROUGH THE SKIN.
–LINDA HOGAN

Hands are one of the most expressive parts of our bodies. They show nervousness by flapping around or by picking fingernails. Clapping, they show appreciation. Fingers snapping, they keep time to a beat. They can help tell a story when they point or draw pictures with movements.

It is good to appreciate our hands. My hands are long and bony. They work hard. They love to pull my body through the water in the summertime or to clear a path through the water for my dive.

Writing exercise: I'll draw a picture of my hand and then describe all the things it does in great detail.

ONCE ONE IS MOLESTED IT'S
VERY HARD TO FEEL CLEAN AGAIN.
–Maya Angelou

My friend's older sister was raped walking home late one night from a party. The experience has been difficult for the whole family. I think they are finding healthy ways to heal, but everybody was really shook-up by this. I was, too.

My Aunt Jane told me that this fear and the possibility of rape is an unfortunate part of being a woman. She thinks self-defense classes help. And being safe: not going out at night to unsafe places, like unchaperoned parties where people are drinking a lot. What we can control, she says, are the situations we choose to put ourselves in.

*I need to do what I can to protect my body
and spirit by making wise choices whenever I can.*

WHINING IS FOR THOSE WHO CAN'T
ASK FOR WHAT THEY WANT.
–MINDY MORGENSTERN

Sometimes asking for what I want seems so simple, but other times it feels hard. What's most important is knowing what I want. This can require some thinking or at least some awareness that I'm unhappy about something.

I was being so crabby toward my little brother and so snotty to my mom. She actually sent me to my room to write in my journal and figure out what was going on. I wrote myself into a description of how mom is always paying special attention to the little guy and never carving out enough time for me. So, when I emerged from my room, I asked if we could plan some time together, and she said she would love to.

If there's something bugging me, I can take the time to figure out what it is and then ask for what I need. This is much more effective and feels better than whining.

PEOPLE OF ALL AGES SEEK WAYS TO FEEL GOOD.

Children spinning around and around on the playground are experimenting with getting high. We all need to do it. In health class we've been talking about healthy ways to get that adrenaline rush or endorphin high.

Physical exercise always works for me. Last summer I went rock climbing. It was challenging and nerve-wracking, and by the end, exhilarating. On a canoe trip my dad and I dove from a tall rock into deep water. That was a rush. So is standing next to a roaring waterfall.

If I ever feel tempted to get high in a dangerous way, I need to remember all the healthier ways I have of feeling good.

WHAT THE OJIBWE CALL THE GIZHE MANIDOO [IS]
THE GREAT AND KIND SPIRIT RESIDING IN ALL THAT LIVES,
AND WHAT THE LAKOTA CALL THE GREAT MYSTERY . . .
–LOUISE ERDRICH

I love the idea of there being a great and kind spirit in all living things. It's a beautiful and simple idea, one I can grasp without fighting or questioning too much. And I love the idea of calling this force the Great Mystery.

There is so much about life that is mysterious. Some questions are too difficult to be answered. Like why do good people die horrible deaths from disease or accidents? How is it there's so much suffering in the world and yet so much beauty?

My questions can be like an offering to the Great Mystery or the Ojibwes' Gizhe Manidoo.

WHAT IS THIS WAR DOING TO MY PARENTS? THEY DON'T
LOOK LIKE MY MOMMY AND DADDY ANYMORE.
–ZLATA FILIPOVIC

Unfortunately, in many parts of the world there are wars and skirmishes going on. We have been studying some of them in history class. It's hard to understand why humans have such a hard time getting along. Yet when I look at my own life, I have a hard time getting along with my brother.

There are scars and wounds that go with war. In her diary, Zlata traced how war aged her parents and shaded their personalities into darker, more burdened versions of their former selves. Perhaps I need to consider how the minor war between me and my brother creates scars as well.

I would like to be a force for peace,
in my own home and in the world.

YOU CAN ASK FORGIVENESS OF OTHERS BUT IN THE END
THE REAL FORGIVENESS IS IN ONE'S OWN SELF.
–MAYA ANGELOU

I have an older cousin who I was really close to for a long time. Then she began to change; she broke promises about spending time with me. One minute she'd be happy to see me, the next she'd put me down. Gradually I spent less and less time with her.

Later I found out she was starting to do a lot of drinking and drugs. She is not doing well in her life now. I struggle with thinking I could have helped prevent this from happening. If only I'd been a better cousin, a smarter cousin. If only I'd talked to her more honestly about her behavior. I'm struggling with how to forgive her and myself.

Sometimes feelings of forgiveness are slow in coming. But I can pray for the willingness to forgive both myself and her.

TODAY IS THE ANNIVERSARY OF
AMELIA EARHART CROSSING THE ATLANTIC.
A DAY TO CELEBRATE FLYING WITH MY DREAMS!

In 1932, way ahead of her time, Earhart was the first woman pilot to cross the Atlantic. I like to think of her courage and her spirit as she soared above that ocean, up there with the eagles and clouds and sunbeams. Flying alone must have been both scary and exhilarating. And she opened the door for women to think of themselves as pilots.

She must have started with a dream, a passion, an interest. And then she had the faith and courage to give her dream wings, physically and symbolically. I hope she had supportive people around her. Encouragement means inspiring courage.

When I think of Amelia Earhart, I am inspired to remember my dreams and to encourage myself to follow them.

I MAY NOT BE RICH IN MATERIAL TERMS, BUT I FEEL
RICH IN SPIRIT. THAT'S ALL THAT COUNTS TO ME.
–AMELIA RUDOLPH

To be rich in spirit. What might that mean? When I think about it, I see an ocean, and tidal waves rolling into shore, surging up from some deep and bottomless source. Happy, joyful, energetic, contented. Ocean waves in the soft moonlight. Ocean waves with sparkles dancing in the brightly lit sun. Ocean waves on cloudy days, full of a deeply thoughtful mood.

To be rich in spirit means to enter deeply into life's emotions. Material girls focus on buying and getting things. The wanting never ends.

Writing exercise: I will write a poem describing what it means to be rich in spirit.

BY BELIEVING IN ME [MY MOTHER] HELPED ME BELIEVE IN
MYSELF. SHE TOLD ME NOTHING WAS IMPOSSIBLE.
–LILLY MELGAR

Sometimes my parents are great at telling me I'm doing well and can accomplish anything I set my mind to. Other times they seem to get busy in their own lives and I don't hear anything very positive from them. But I have found that if I just gently remind them by saying something like, "What do you think about how I'm playing soccer these days?" they usually kick in with what I need to hear.

I had tests a couple of weeks ago, and the night before, my mom said, "You're a very bright girl. All you need is a good night of sleep and a healthy breakfast, and you'll do great." The next morning before I delved into the first test, I found myself saying almost the exact same words to myself. They definitely helped.

*When someone speaks positively about me, I can carry their
words inside and repeat them to myself when I need to.
Encouraging words heal and strengthen me.*

AND LIFE MUST REALLY HAVE JOY.
IT'S SUPPOSED TO BE FUN.
–BARBARA BUSH

I really do have a good time with my friends. And I can see that my parents have fun with their friends, too, although they seem to have less time for play than I do. Lately my friends and I have fun meeting at the neighborhood coffee shop or going to the mall together. It's really just hanging out with each other that counts. We talk a lot, and I've noticed how much we laugh when we're together.

I'm grateful for the companionship, because it makes my life warmer. Laughing always lifts my spirits.

I am grateful today for the ways that talking, walking, and laughing with friends make my life a fun and joyful one.

DON'T LET OTHERS DEFINE YOU AND
TELL YOU WHAT YOU LIKE OR DON'T LIKE,
OR WHAT YOU CAN OR CAN'T DO.
–MARSHA KINDER

I think where girls my age are most likely to mess up is with boys. It's really a whole new world, even though some of us have been going out with boys for a while. My mom says the male-female thing is always tricky, but you get better at it the older you get. She says really, you just come to know yourself better.

I know when something feels right to me and when it doesn't. And I know when I feel pressured. There's no need for me to get pressured to do things that don't feel right: drugs, sex, or driving with someone who's been drinking. I need to think about how I will feel about my decisions in the long run.

There are long-term consequences to my decisions. After all, my choices become part of who I am.

WRITING IS A TOOL OF TRANSFORMATION
AND CAN SHINE THE LIGHT ON THE INSIDE,
DISPELLING DARKNESS, TAKING US THROUGH
EXTERNAL LAYERS, BRINGING US CLOSER TO OUR SOULS.
–HILLARY CARLIP

The other day I was being really snappy with my brothers and dad. I didn't really know why. Finally my dad sent me to my room. There, I listened to my favorite CD and wrote in my journal. I realized as I wrote that I was feeling sad for my friend Yolanda, whose boyfriend broke up with her. I hate to see her feeling sad because she is such a cool person.

I also realized I'm anxious about an upcoming test in math and tryouts for the school play. Also I'm tired. I'm a very busy girl, and sometimes the stream of activities stresses me out. So sitting down to write made me more aware of all these feelings and helped me understand why I was so on edge. When I came out of my room, I told Mom, and she was very compassionate.

Writing exercise: I will sit and write about the feelings beneath my actions. Self-awareness is an important step in my personal growth.

THE FAMILY IS THE BUILDING BLOCK FOR
WHATEVER SOLIDARITY THERE IS IN SOCIETY.
–JILL RUCKELSHAUS

Solidarity means working together. The other day I was in a really good mood, and when my dad announced it was yard cleaning day, instead of my usual complaining mode, I got into it. I raked and bagged. My dad and I sang old Beatles songs as we worked. My brothers and mother came and helped after they got back from my brother's baseball practice.

When we took a mid-afternoon lemonade break, the yard really looked good. We all felt pleased with our work. I've had the same feeling at times when we've all pitched in to help clean inside as well.

Even though I usually resist the idea, helping around the house is important, and it does feel good to contribute to a cleaner house and yard.

I LOVE TO GO SOMEWHERE WHERE
THERE'S NO SOUND EXCEPT THE WIND AND TREES.
–RENEE ZELLWEGER

One of my favorite places in the world is my grandma's cabin. When I can sit on the dock and listen to the wind roar or the light breeze sift through the trees around me, it is heavenly.

There are also places in the city I love for the same reasons. The park near my house has a beautiful stand of blue spruce and oak trees. The wind creates such different moods as it moves through spruce needles and oak leaves. Sometimes the wind soothes me and sometimes it energizes me. The wind always reminds me of a bigger picture than my own small life.

*Today I will listen to the wind,
and hear what it has to say to me.*

WHEN YOU'RE JUMPING SO HIGH FOR SOMETHING
SO FAR UP IN THE SKY, YOU HAVE TO KNOW THAT
THERE IS DEFINITELY SOMEONE THERE WHO CAN CATCH
YOU, SOMEONE WHO KNOWS HOW TO CATCH YOU
AND WHEN. MOM IS JUST THAT WAY.
—PICABO STREET

In spite of all the difficulties I have with my mom, I know she and my dad will be the first ones to catch me if I fall. Or I should say, when I fall. They really are there for me. Only sometimes I get into pushing them away. I'm not sure why, except that I'm trying to carve out my own path. Most of my friends are fighting their parents, too.

So today I want to think about how much I appreciate my parents being the solid, rock-like foundations of my life. Even my friends whose parents are divorced know that both parents really love them. And my friend Ellie, whose dad disappeared when she was young, has an uncle who is like a father for her.

I will make a gesture of appreciation to my parents and other loving adults, the ones I know are ready to catch me if and when I fall.

MEMORIES, MEMORIES, MEMORIES.

On Memorial Day weekend, my family sometimes goes to the cemetery to visit the graves of an aunt of mine who died in a car accident and a great uncle who died in World War II.

This trip is always sad, but it also feels good. The cemetery is usually lush and green and beautiful. Sometimes cemeteries look lonely to me; but on this weekend, more flowers and people arrive. It makes me think how important it is to remember people—those who have died and those who are still living.

Writing exercise: What do I remember about the people I have loved who have died or who live far away from me? I will remember them by writing my memories of them.

WE MAY NOT BE ABLE TO CHANGE AN OUTER
CIRCUMSTANCE, BUT WE DO HAVE A CHOICE IN
HOW WE PERCEIVE IT AND REACT TO IT.
A POSITIVE ATTITUDE IS A POWERFUL THING.
–HILLARY CARLIP

My friend Shaiwan did not make the first cut on the soccer team. The same week, Lindsay's mom had to go to the hospital with near-fatal pneumonia. I watched and supported both of these friends, who could have really bummed out.

Instead, after a good cry on my shoulder and her mother's, Shaiwan decided she loves the game of soccer and the exercise, so she's already looking forward to playing with some of our other friends on the junior varsity team. Lindsay has been helping her dad and her younger sister, and she visits her mother every day. She is so happy her mom's okay and getting better. She hasn't wasted any time asking Why her? Why me? Instead, she is experiencing a special kind of family closeness.

When life throws something difficult my way,
I can meet it head on with all my positive spirit.

THE END OF THE SCHOOL YEAR IS AN IMPORTANT MILESTONE IN MY LIFE.

Each year seems like such an accomplishment. Freshman year meant I survived being the youngest in the high school. And each year brings me new challenges, with senior year bringing especially big ones. You can see it on the faces of the seniors: a real feeling of jubilation and accomplishment, and yet a sort of sadness, too. Endings are sad. Next year will always be different, and each of us may miss something from the previous year.

At the end of the school year, I like to think about my accomplishments. What did I learn this year? Usually a lot, but it's good to think about specifics. I also like to think about the high and low points.

Writing exercise: I will write in my journal about all the lessons I've learned this year.

JUNE

THANK-YOUS ARE BEST IF THEY ARE SPOKEN, WRITTEN, PAINTED, OR DANCED.

This time of year I have so many teachers to thank. I used to think, Oh, they know they've done a good job. But last year I wrote a special thank-you to my English teacher because she had coached me on writing, and the writing helped me through that difficult period when my dad moved out and Brian broke up with me.

I wrote this teacher a poem and drew and colored all over it. When I gave it to her, she got tears in her eyes. She told me, "It's moments like this that keep me teaching." I was so glad I took the time to let her know how much I appreciated all she'd done for me.

Even a simple but heartfelt thank-you
means a lot to teachers.

I RAP OUT A SENTENCE IN MY
NOTEBOOK AND I FEEL BETTER.
–FLORIDA SCOTT-MAXWELL

Most of my friends keep journals and I do, too. It really helps to sit down and write when I'm upset or down. There's something about putting my questions and feelings on paper that both helps to get them out of my body and helps make them clearer for me. Sometimes I'm surprised by what I write; I actually learn more about myself by writing things down.

It's also fun to write when I'm feeling great. I write about my accomplishments and good times and talks with friends. It's helpful to look back and read these entries when I'm down. They always brighten me up.

Writing exercise: I will take time today to scrawl or rap out a sentence or a page. It will help me feel better.

ENJOY YOUR ACHIEVEMENTS AS WELL AS YOUR PLANS.
–DESIDERATA

Both my achievements and my plans keep me going. Yet I'm often too busy to stop and think and honor either one. With this school year drawing to a close, it's been good for me to think about all I've done. I've gotten good grades and learned a lot. I've played in band and jazz band all year, and my flute playing is so much better than it was in the fall.

I passed a very difficult level in skating and played well on my soccer team. And I was in the school play. When I stop and look, I can see I'm doing a lot. It's time to pat myself on the back. And to remember my dreams for the next year and for my future.

It's good to stop once in a while and notice all that I'm doing. My future plans beckon to me, like lights in the distance

I NEED TO LOVE MY MOTHER, EVEN WHEN IT'S HARD.

I seem to be in a phase when I'm having a hard time with my mother. She bugs me. Although to be honest, what bugs me the most is when she says no to something I want to do. I tend to fight her No's, which makes things between us even harder. And then when something else comes up that I'd really like to ask her about, I'm so mad at her I can't.

This is such a difficult relationship for me, and it's the same with most of my friends and their mothers. But I do have a lot questions about boys and other things that I think she could help with. And she really does a lot for me. If she weren't around, I know I'd really miss her.

How can I open my heart more toward my mother, toward the part of me that still needs her love in my daily life?

I WILL WRITE YOU A LETTER,
JUNE DAY. DEAR JUNE FIFTH,
YOU'RE ALL IN GREEN . . .
–JAMES SCHUYLER

Around this time of year, everything shifts. School is almost over and I can feel myself perched at the edge of summer's excitement. At this edge I can look backward and forward and see more clearly than usual.

I want to write a letter to today from this vantage point, this uncluttered horizon. And I want to begin it by describing today, its colors and scents and small beauties and worries. From my bedroom window or my backyard or my front step, what do I see and hear and smell? What can I feel in the air? And what do I see of the year behind me and the summer ahead?

*Writing exercise: I will write a letter to this day
as if the day itself were my best friend.*

GRADUATION IS A MIXTURE OF BEGINNINGS AND ENDINGS.

My cousin is graduating this year, and she says it's incredibly exciting, yet she finds herself crying easily. She has done so well in high school, both as a student and with all of her other activities, and she's excited about the college she has chosen. But it will be like starting all over again: full of possibility and uncharted territory. Very exciting, somewhat scary. Full of new friends and the sadness of not seeing much of her old friends.

When it's my turn, I want to feel proud of all the hard work I've put into high school. I want to feel close to my friends and know we've done it together.

Endings are a time to appreciate my completed part of the journey and to feel inspired about the next part of my journey.

I DO NOT LIKE THE IDEA OF HAPPINESS—
IT IS TOO MOMENTARY—I WOULD SAY THAT I WAS
ALWAYS BUSY AND INTERESTED IN SOMETHING—
INTEREST HAS MORE MEANING THAN HAPPINESS.
—GEORGIA O'KEEFFE

This statement by an artist whose work I love made me think. I love her paintings of flowers: they are so beautiful, I want to enter them. I'm intrigued by the idea of interest being more enduring than happiness. It's true that happiness seems to come and go. But being interested in something specific in life can give me long-term contentment.

It's made me think about my interests. I have many: sports, music, drama, studying. I like to think about how some of these will be with me all of my life. I'd like to be like my mom and still be into sports when I'm older—she runs and rollerblades. I'd like to be like my aunt, who still plays piano.

I will honor my interests and remember that they can help me feel focused today and for years to come.

WE ARE RICH ONLY THROUGH WHAT WE GIVE.
–ANNE-SOPHIE SWETCHINE

Lately we have been talking in history class about how there have always been many people living in poverty. Our history teacher brought it even closer to home with statistics of the numbers of people in our own city who are homeless. My parents recently made my brothers and me help out at our church's outreach ministry. We spent a morning giving vouchers for shoes to families with young children.

It was an eye-opener to me. First to see children who have to stand in line to get a pair of much-needed shoes. And then to see how happy they were to get them. Such appreciation. It felt good to do something to help out people with far less than I have, but I also learned about appreciating what I have from them.

Writing exercise: I will think and write about some things I take for granted. What are some ways I can deepen my gratitude for these things?

I RESTORE MYSELF WHEN I'M ALONE.
A CAREER IS BORN IN PUBLIC–TALENT IN PRIVACY.
–MARILYN MONROE

Some of my most talented friends are the ones who don't mind spending time alone. In fact, they like it. Jessica is an amazing reader, and she is smart and a good writer. She often sits for a whole afternoon or evening just reading. Yolanda practices piano for hours: she can play jazz and classical. I know she is really good, but I also know she puts in a lot of time practicing.

Being alone is not my strong suit. I don't usually choose it because I'm so social. But when solitude gets forced on me by my parents or circumstances, I remember how good it feels. It gives me time to focus on the quiet skills I want to develop: playing piano and writing and drawing. Sometimes I get so busy I forget to carve out time for these things.

*I need time for the quiet activities that help me feel good
and develop my skills–the ones that feed my soul.*

FATHER'S DAY IS SPECIAL.

My dad takes me fishing. He taught me how to bait a hook, how to feel the difference between a snag and a fish on the line. Most of all, he taught me to love being out in a boat on the water. It's so peaceful there.

So I'm making a big card for him in the shape of a fish and writing the things I've learned from him all over it. Besides fishing, he's taught me how to love classical music and great books and kindness to other people.

My friends and I are all doing something special for our dads (or stepdads or favorite uncles) this year. They deserve it.

IT'S IMPORTANT FOR GIRLS TO EXPLORE THE IMPACT THE
CULTURE HAS ON THEIR GROWTH AND DEVELOPMENT....
ONCE GIRLS UNDERSTAND THE EFFECTS OF CULTURE
ON THEIR LIVES, THEY CAN FIGHT BACK.
–MARY PIPHER

My social studies teacher, Ms. Grace, has developed
a whole section about the messages we get from the
media about being male and female. We looked at teen
magazines, MTV videos, and popular movies. I was
shocked how many of the messages are about females
being powerful only if we look good. And smoking is
made to look so alluring. Sexuality is made to look easy,
not complicated, like it really is.

No wonder some of my friends starve themselves, no
wonder we all worry so much about clothes and
makeup. But studying this made me want to fight back
and not get so sucked in. It made me want to stand up
and *shout*, "I'm more than just a body!"

I am becoming more conscious of all messages
directed at us girls and how they affect me.
This awareness gives me power to make more choices.

THERE ARE MANY POSITIVE,
HEALTHY WAYS TO FIND PLEASURE.

Some of my friends' parents drink a lot. My dad doesn't drink anymore, but my mom has a glass of wine or two when they go out for dinner or have friends over. But some of my friend's parents drink enough that when they come home at night, they cannot drive safely.

This is confusing for some of us who are just starting to deal with drug use. My dad keeps saying there are so many ways to feel good in this world that drinking isn't necessary at my age. Then he adds: "Not to mention, illegal, unsafe, and against your athletic and our house rules." I do like the idea of finding lots of other ways to feel good and to have fun.

Writing exercise: I will write out five to ten healthy, clean, 'right' ways I can experience a natural high.

THE DAY CAME WHEN THE RISK IT TOOK
TO REMAIN TIGHT IN A BUD BECAME MORE PAINFUL
THAN THE RISK IT TOOK TO BLOSSOM.
–ANAIS NIN

Sometimes I feel shy. Yolanda is really shy. I think a little bit of shyness is normal. But one day I realized my shyness was keeping me from saying what I thought and felt in my group of friends and in my classes. One day in English class I knew the answer; I was one of the few who had read the assignment. I was feeling hesitant to raise my hand at first, but after a while it drove me crazy to stay quiet.

So up went my hand. The teacher was impressed with my answer and my knowledge. And it felt good not to carry the answer around inside me all day, quiet and hidden.

Blossoming, in small and large ways, often requires stepping out of my comfort zone.

A GOOD LAUGH OVERCOMES MORE
DIFFICULTIES AND DISSIPATES MORE DARK
CLOUDS THAN ANY OTHER ONE THING.
–LAURA INGALLS WILDER

Two people in my life make me laugh a lot: my friend Jessica and my dad. The things Jessica says and the way she says them just cracks me up. She can also do great imitations of funny people: comedians and teachers and classmates.

Dad helps me to laugh at myself. When I'm in a growly mood he calls me Stormcloud and says, "Don't smile, whatever you do, don't smile . . ." But he says it in a such a nice teasing way that eventually I smile, and then I laugh. He helps me laugh at myself, because usually nothing in my life is quite that serious.

I'll remember that laughing easily is good for my soul!

SADNESS IS MORE OR LESS LIKE A HEAD COLD—
WITH PATIENCE, IT PASSES.
–BARBARA KINGSOLVER

My parents usually get along so well, but they had a big argument the other day, and it made me feel sad for days. The thing about feeling sad, or bad in any way, I guess, is it seems as if it's going to last forever. But it doesn't. Nothing lasts forever.

My sadness passed in a couple of days, helped by seeing my mom and dad getting along again. They assured me that they love each other, but had had a big disagreement. It helped to hear that. I think the other reason feeling sad is like a cold is because you have to let it out a bit, just like you have to blow your nose with a cold. When I talked to my dad and mom about my feelings and wrote in my journal, that helped to lighten my feelings.

!

*When I'm feeling sad, I'm like a cloud that
needs moisture released. The wind soon
blows the cloud away and brings on sunshine.*

IN THE WORLD THERE IS A BALANCE OF
GOOD AND BAD, SO WHEN A BAD DAY COMES,
KNOW THAT A GOOD DAY IS JUST AROUND THE CORNER.
–MARGARET SULLIVAN, AGE 17

I was thinking about the children's book, *Alexander and the Terrible Horrible No Good Day* the other day. All my favorite clothes were in the laundry basket and dirty. I had left my hairbrush and my shoes in the car and had to go get them before I was really awake. Then I missed my bus and had to run like crazy to the next bus stop. While I ran, I broke the strap on my backpack, and my books fell all over the sidewalk.

At school some of my friends were leaving me out, or at least I thought so. I felt off-balance all day until I walked in the door and told my mom and dad my troubles. It was a comfort to land at home and be accepted just as I was. My next day was much better.

A bad day reminds me of the comfort of my family.
A bad day is usually followed by a good day.

EACH DAY I LOOK FOR A KERNEL OF EXCITEMENT.
IN THE MORNING I SAY, "WHAT IS MY EXCITING
THING FOR TODAY?" THEN, I DO THE DAY.
–BARBARA JORDAN

My aunt says she wakes up every morning and thanks God for the new day. My cousin Rachel says she lights a candle and writes in her journal every morning. I have decided I can lie in bed and listen to the classical music station and think about the best parts of the day ahead of me. There's always something special or that I'm excited about.

My neighbor who struggles with depression lost the ability to find anything to look forward to in a day. She was able to get help. I've heard her talking about it with my mom. This makes me grateful for the ability to appreciate something in each day and to be aware that when I or one of my friends can't do that, it may be time to get help.

I can practice waking in the morning and anticipating
at least one great thing about the day ahead.

I THINK SELF-AWARENESS IS PROBABLY THE MOST
IMPORTANT THING TOWARDS BEING A CHAMPION.
–Billie Jean King

Sometimes I can't figure out why I'm acting a certain way. It may be that I'm crabby or mean to my brother or that I'm eating a lot or always looking for the boys at school. When how I'm acting feels a bit funny inside or I find myself wondering why, then it's time to slow down. I figure it out by talking to a good friend or occasionally to my mom or dad. What helps even more is to write in my journal. Sometimes things come out that surprise me, things that help me understand myself.

One day I wanted to eat junk food all day. When I started writing, I realized two things: I was really tired and needed a long night of sleep, and I was upset about an argument I had had with Teresa. My anxiety took the form of nervous eating. Sleep and a good talk helped me feel much calmer, which changed how I was behaving and what I was craving.

Writing exercise: I will take time to sit down and write about any behaviors I'm questioning and to write about the feelings underlying those behaviors.

INTUITION IS WHEN WE KNOW BUT WE DON'T KNOW
HOW WE KNOW—IT'S KNOWING FROM THE INSIDE OUT.
–NANCY ROSANOFF

I actually feel a shift in my stomach when I know something is right or wrong for me. Like when I first met Angie, I felt so strongly that this was someone I should know. She and I have become great friends, and in many ways she helps me be a better person.

When Brian invited Angie and me over to his house on a Friday night, I had a bad feeling about it. He said his parents would be home, but when we walked in the door, they weren't, and the guys were already drinking a lot. I had a bad feeling right away and thank goodness Angie did, too. We made an excuse, like we had to go pick up Yolanda, and then we never went back. I've heard some bad stories about the girls who stayed there that night, and I'm glad I ducked out of the way.

My insides, my gut, my heart are often wiser than my brain.
My job is to listen to what my body is saying.

NORMAL DAY, LET ME BE AWARE OF THE TREASURE
YOU ARE. LET ME NOT PASS YOU BY IN QUEST OF
SOME RARE AND PERFECT TOMORROW.
–MARY HEAN IRION

Last week I was miserably sick for three days. When I finally woke up feeling good, I appreciated just being able to do all the normal stuff I do so much. It felt great to be able to eat breakfast again, to hop on my bike and ride to soccer practice with Lizzie, to hang out in the evening with my family.

The day felt special to me even though it was ordinary. This taught me that if I am consciously grateful every day for being healthy, alive, and here in the middle of my life, then every day is special.

Let me appreciate fully the beauty of every ordinary day.

LIGHT
IS AN INVITATION
TO HAPPINESS
–MARY OLIVER

June brings the summer solstice. I read in the paper that at the North and South Poles, where the sun doesn't rise at all in winter, the summer solstice brings sunlight twenty-four hours a day.

I like to think about that as June 21st approaches. It makes the day a special one for me. I like to think of it as a day where the darkest parts of many of us, of our world in general, receive light and warmth. It seems like a good day to be festive, to organize a gathering of friends or family, to be thankful for the light and happiness in my life.

Writing exercise: I will celebrate the light in my life by writing about it: how light shines in my bedroom window or in a favorite room in my house; how light makes the willow tree green; how certain people bring light into my life.

HAPPINESS IS A GIFT. BUT IT CANNOT BE GIVEN TO
YOU BY OTHER PEOPLE, YOU GIVE IT TO YOURSELF.
–JACQUELINE KEHOE

What makes me happy? This is a good question to ask once in a while. It's especially good to ask in this season of light. In ancient times, people danced around fires and made promises about the days ahead. Shakespeare wrote a play about this time of love and play: *A Midsummer Night's Dream.*

Certain songs make me happy, as do skating and having time alone with either one of my parents. Sleepovers also feel good, and so does smelling and eating my mom's homemade coffee cake. Writing in my journal and drawing always feel good, in a contented way. I wonder why I don't spend more time doing the things in my life which bring me happiness, contentedness, or joy?

I can make a conscious effort to do something every day that makes me happy.

As stewards of this planet, we need to make sure that we don't damage it. If we can, we must leave it better than when we came.
–Sandra Day O'Connor

When we study the environment in class, I remember how important each of our actions is. Small things, like not littering and picking up litter when you see it, make a difference. When I went canoeing last summer with our class, it broke my heart to see garbage in the wilderness. Who could disrespect such beauty?

The planet is my home and deserves to be treated with kindness and respect. No lazy moments of dropping a wrapper.

I am a steward of this planet, and I need to keep it clean and loved for the next generation.

LITERACY MEANS LIBERATION.
–SEPTIMA CLARK

My English teacher says that the more we read, the more doors will open to us. It is amazing how many books he knows: he is so wise, and part of how he understands so many things is through his knowledge of books, stories, and beautiful language.

Every time I choose to read rather than watch TV, I deepen my knowledge of the world and the human heart. I would much rather be wise than eat junk-food wisdom on TV. Summer reading is the best!

How I spend time creates me. Today I will make wise choices, choices to deepen and enlarge my heart.

I BELIEVE IN BUTTERFLIES AND QUIET SONGS, IN EARLY
SUNRISES AND THE STARS AT NIGHT. I BELIEVE IN THE
MOON DURING THE DAY. I BELIEVE IN THE OCEAN.
–BOBBI HERVIN

What we believe matters. My friends come from all different backgrounds and have different beliefs. Gita was born in India and believes in the power of sunrises and nonviolence. She is a great admirer of Gandhi. Yolanda's family believes deeply in the power of music–I've been to their church service, and their songs are so inspiring and uplifting that I floated for days afterward.

I feel like I'm going through some changes about my beliefs, some questioning. My dad and mom say they've gone through different stages of what and whom they believe in. They both say it's important to think about this.

Writing exercise: I will write a list of
what and whom I believe in.

I AM CONFIDENT IN MYSELF BECAUSE OF WHAT I
DO AND WHO I AM. I CAN DO MARVELOUS THINGS!
–KALEY DARGA

I always think of that scene from The Sound of Music in which Julie Andrews swings her guitar and sings at the top of her lungs, "I am confident . . ." When I have to be especially strong, I call upon that image and sing those words to myself.

Every once in a while my dad or mom sits down with me and tells me how amazing I am: how hard I work at things, how many talents I have and am developing. The word confidence means to trust in oneself. Their belief in me helps me trust myself.

*I trust that life is good and that I can be
and do anything I really feel like.*

IF YOU'RE NOT PART OF THE SOLUTION
THEN YOU'RE PART OF THE PROBLEM.

My dad gets involved in political caucuses because he says the people we elect affect the laws that govern us. He is always asking me questions about politics in our city and state and country. He wants me to think about these things, and when the time comes, to be an informed voter.

One of the issues I care a lot about is the environment. Companies that pollute our air and our groundwater hurt all of us for their monetary gain. It drives me crazy to see garbage in our parks and wilderness areas, so I always pick it up. I try not to waste water, gas, and paper products.

*What am I doing today to make our world
a safer, cleaner, and better place?*

EACH FRIEND REPRESENTS A WORLD IN US,
A WORLD POSSIBLY NOT BORN UNTIL THEY ARRIVE.
–ANAIS NIN

One of the great things about friends is how each one brings out a different part of me. I can be really silly and goofy with Keesha–we seem to tickle each other's senses of humor. Yolanda, because she is so good on the piano, always makes me want to practice so I can play what she is playing. Angie is my workout partner–we run together and keep each other in shape. We're competitive with each other but this makes us both a little better in the athletic department.

I'm grateful for my friends and how, each in her own way helps me be a better and stronger person.

Writing exercise: I will take time to write about how each of my friends is a positive influence in my life. Anyone who is not a positive influence is probably not a very good friend.

THERE ARE SOME THINGS YOU LEARN
BEST IN CALM AND SOME IN STORM.
–WILLA CATHER

I've been noticing there are different ways of learning things about myself. Getting better at liking myself seems to be a skill that is growing slowly, a little each day. I tacked up mottoes on my mirror and bedroom wall, such as "I like myself for all that I am and all that I can be."

I was hanging with this boy in our class for a while, but I always came away feeling bad. He complimented other girls, making me feel bad, and sometimes he put me down in a humorous way. One day it hit me: Why hang with someone whose company makes me question myself and feel bad? I could literally feel a shift inside my body, especially my heart and gut. I stopped hanging out with him that very day.

I will pay attention today to what I am learning in quiet, steady ways and what I am learning in stormier ways.

KEEP A GRATEFUL JOURNAL. EVERY NIGHT,
LIST FIVE THINGS THAT YOU ARE GRATEFUL FOR.
WHAT IT WILL BEGIN TO DO IS CHANGE YOUR
PERSPECTIVE OF YOUR DAY AND YOUR LIFE.
–OPRAH WINFREY

It is incredibly easy to notice what I don't have instead of all that I do. I have my dad's parents who raised a big family without much money. When I ask my grandparents if this was hard, they say it was in some ways, but they always had great faith that God would help them through it. My grandmother is quick to point out that they were all healthy and that all eight of their children turned out well.

Both Grandma and Grandpa focus more on what went well, on the gifts of physical health and loving relationships. Dad says they were always able to do that. I think this is pretty amazing and inspiring.

Writing exercise: Every night for a week, I will list five things I am grateful for and see how this shifts my perspective.

JULY

> READING IS TO THE MIND WHAT
> EXERCISE IS TO THE BODY.
> –JOSEPH ADDISON

Remember the game *Trivial Pursuit*? My uncle Toby was a genius at that game, and when we divided into teams, everyone wanted to be on his side. He always won. When I asked him how he could know about so many things, he said he has always loved learning. He was a good student because he read voraciously, studied, and really wanted to know about history and different cultures, about how science and math connected.

My uncle can talk to anybody about anything. He is passionately curious about this world. He writes a column for the newspaper and runs his own business. I admire him and can see that his love for knowing things made him take his education seriously. He is like a light shining now into my life, telling me to read and learn all I can, because the world is a fascinating place. In the summer, I love to have a stack of books in my room and to trade books with my friends.

What I read today can cast a light into all of my tomorrows.

AND FORGET NOT THAT THE EARTH LONGS
TO FEEL YOUR BARE FEET AND THE WIND LONGS
TO PLAY WITH YOUR HAIR.
–KAHLIL GIBRAN

When warm weather arrives, I love to take my shoes off and glide through the smooth green grass with my bare feet. At our cabin, my feet soak up warmth from granite rock and sand on the beach. I love the feel of the sun, transformed by the earth beneath me, warming me from the bottom of my feet on up. My bare feet flipping their way through water also sends me.

It seems like spring and summer, after a cold winter, invite us all into a special celebration. I see people in their gardens or kids out playing in their yards. Our Creator provides us with many simple pleasures.

*When I celebrate the feel of grass or granite
beneath my feet, I am celebrating the gift of life.*

When I look at the kids training today. . .
I can tell which ones are going to do well.
It's not necessarily the ones who have the
most natural talent or who fall the least.
Sometimes it's the kids who fall the most
and keep pulling themselves up and trying again.
–Michelle Kwan

I'm back to taking piano lessons again after not taking for over a year. Several of my friends are much better than I am, and I often feel discouraged. I worry I don't have enough talent. Then I have to remember that I keep being drawn back to it. When my friends play, I want to be able to play that well.

When a song looks like Greek to me, I need to remember that after a few days' practice, I will figure out all the notes, and after a few more days' practice, I can begin to play smoothly and with feeling. Learning something new requires patience and persistence.

Writing exercise: I will write about where I need patience and persistence in my life right now. What daily steps are necessary to bring me closer to my goals?

THE RIGHT WAY IS NOT ALWAYS THE POPULAR
AND EASY WAY. STANDING FOR RIGHT WHEN IT IS
UNPOPULAR IS A TRUE TEST OF MORAL CHARACTER.
–MARGARET CHASE SMITH

There's a very popular boy in my class: he's athletic, good looking, and smart. He can also be mean. Sometimes he makes fun of people, one girl in our class in particular. Everybody goes along with it, because everybody wants to be liked by him.

The other day he started going into his routine. We were in science class, and no one was stepping forward to be this girl's lab partner. He began to crack jokes under his breath. Suddenly I felt so offended by his meanness that I stepped forward to be her lab partner. I noticed the palm of my hands were sweaty–it was a scary thing to do, because I risked being made fun of. But I'll sleep better tonight.

!

*When something is nudging me and feels wrong,
I can take a deep breath, dive into my store of courage,
and take action. Doing the right thing is far better for
me in the long run than doing the popular thing.*

> DREAMS COME A SIZE TOO BIG
> SO THAT WE CAN GROW INTO THEM.
> –Josie Bisset

Jessica wants to be a dancer in New York City, and David wants to write plays for Broadway. Gita wants to be a composer and is already writing songs for the piano. Me? Playing college soccer and becoming a novelist are my current dreams.

The thing about dreams is they give you a golden light to walk toward. Even when I'm tired and want to skip soccer practice or skip a homework assignment, it's the dream that helps me get up the energy to do what I need to do. I like having friends who dream big, too. I can tell this is good for me.

Inspiration is good fuel for daily discipline.
Dreams inspire me, and my friends' dreams inspire me, too.

HEALTH IS NOT SIMPLY THE ABSENCE OF SICKNESS.
–HANNAH GREEN

Being healthy is important to me, but I don't always put the pieces of being healthy together. There's physical health, and for that, exercise, eating well, not getting too stressed out, and getting plenty of sleep are important. I get lots of exercise, sometimes not enough rest, and I can get on real bad eating jags. I know I feel better when I'm eating a lot of fruits and vegetables and drinking lots of water, but I have a weakness for sugar.

Another part of health is expressing my emotions so they don't get all bottled up inside me. When I'm talking with my friends or my mom or writing in my journal, I'm doing well. When I'm taking care of my physical health and emotional health, I'm a much happier person.

What can I do today to be healthy?

MY MEANS OF EMPOWERMENT HAS ALWAYS BEEN TO
SEARCH OUT WONDERFUL FRIENDS, PEOPLE WHO
BELIEVE IN ME, WHO HELP ME BELIEVE IN MYSELF.
–SANDY WARSHAW

I sometimes think about how lonely my life would be without my friends. Because they know me so well, they keep me honest. They also encourage me. "You're good at that," Lindsay says. Or "Why wouldn't you try out for the play? You have such a good singing voice." Or "Sign up for this science project with me, and we'll learn a lot and have a good time together."

The teams I'm on are fun because of my teammates. We challenge each other, but there's a camaraderie that feels more important. Life without friends would be lonely: with friends, there's warmth and sharing that make me a better person.

I appreciate my friends by letting them know how much I like and care about them, by complimenting them or helping them out.

It's 5% TALENT, 15% SKILL AND 80% HANGING IN THERE.
–LUCY LAWLESS

There's a senior in our school who is breaking all the records for girls' hockey. She's the lead scorer and lead assistant to scores. It is so fun to watch her skate: she is fast and fluid on the ice. I talked to her one day and found out that when she was in seventh grade, she had a lot of back trouble from a bad fall. She wondered if she would ever be able to play well again.

She still has to do special back exercises to keep her back strong and limber. She has to stretch before and after every workout and every game. She is incredibly disciplined, but she knows if she doesn't do it, her body will pay. She thinks it's this discipline, this need to overcome a weakness, which made her strong.

*I can honor my interests and passions in life
by being persistent and disciplined.
These are more important than raw talent.*

> TO HAVE IDEAS IS TO GATHER FLOWERS;
> TO THINK, IS TO WEAVE THEM INTO GARLANDS.
> –ANNE-SOPHIE SWETCHINE

I have lots of ideas. Lately, they are ideas for poems and song lyrics, but other times I've had different ideas. Right now, I'm spending some time every week writing these poems and songs in my journal. That's the part that feels like gathering flowers.

My English teacher says the high school literary magazine is looking for poems, and my friend who plays guitar wants to write music to go with my lyrics. It's scary stepping out into the light like that and putting my fledgling talent on display, but I have nothing to lose and lots to gain. So I'm going to think of the next step as making a garland out of my flowers, putting my talents to use, and expressing them.

Writing exercise: What ideas have been floating in my mind lately? I will spend time jotting down my ideas and then think about what I might do with them.

DON'T GET HUNG UP ON A SNAG IN THE STREAM,
MY DEAR. SNAGS ALONE ARE NOT SO DANGEROUS—
IT'S THE DEBRIS THAT CLINGS TO THEM THAT MAKES
THE TROUBLE. PULL YOURSELF LOOSE AND GO ON.
—ANNE SHANNON MONROE

Recently, two of my friends hit snags. Yolanda didn't make the varsity track team as we all thought she would, and Lindsay's boyfriend broke up with her. She wasn't expecting that at all. Yolanda was pretty low for a couple of days, but she said her mother sat her down and talked to her about people with real problems. And after she thought about it, she decided to stay in track and keep training because she loves it. Lindsay, too, was depressed for about a week. Then she said she realized how happy she was to be back spending more time with her girlfriends. We're all taking special care of her, inviting her to do things all the time. Neither one spent too much time hung up on her disappointment. Both picked up to carry on, and I admire this.

*I hope that when I hit snags, I can move on
and not get hung up on them. My friends are good
role models for me and we help each other keep moving.*

> THE SPIRITUAL REALM IS THE SOURCE OF ALL
> THE OTHERS. . . THERE YOU ARE DEEPENED AND
> GIVEN THE PATTERN AS WELL AS THE PURPOSE THAT
> GUIDES YOUR HIGHER SERVICE IN THE WORLD.
> –JEAN HOUSTON

My Sunday School teacher had us write about the times when we feel most spiritual. I have a CD of classical music called Inner Peace, which my father gave me for my birthday a few years ago. When I listen to this at night in bed, waves of peacefulness wash over me. Along with waves of peacefulness come waves of hope. Any problems I'm struggling with suddenly seem like they will work out okay.

My mom says that sometimes church or a long peaceful run outside in beautiful weather makes her feel this way. Dad says being near water does it for him. He feels soothed and grateful for the beauty of this earth and his life.

It's important for me to dip into the spiritual realm of my life on a regular basis–through nature, music, or church.

DISCOVERING THE SPIRITUAL CENTER WILL LEAD
TO INTERNAL FREEDOM AND CONFIDENCE.
–Adele Wilcox

Spiritual center? What does that mean? My parents are making us go to Sunday School. And I find I really like the questions that come up there for discussion. There's a lot of focus on justice, on thinking about less privileged people and children all over the world, and on how God can help us in our daily lives.

I can see how having a strong relationship with God, however I or anyone else imagines God, can be a comforting thing. I feel like I'm just beginning this road and have a lot to learn. But I do sense how believing in something or Someone can give me comfort and strength.

It's important to think about what is at the spiritual center of my life. Discovering this will make my life stronger and better.

REMOVE THOSE 'I WANT YOU TO LIKE ME'
STICKERS FROM YOUR FOREHEAD AND, INSTEAD,
PLACE THEM WHERE THEY TRULY WILL DO
THE MOST GOOD—ON YOUR MIRROR!
—SUSAN JEFFERS

Lately I have noticed that my friends and I will do things just to get a boy to notice us or even to gain prestige among our group. Lizzie is wearing more makeup than she should—she's starting to look ridiculous. Cassie can be mean just to get a laugh out of others, and then she feels bad later. Sometimes I don't stand up for what I think is right, just so I can fit in. I always end up regretting that.

Saying to myself every day that I like me would be much better. I like the idea of working on being a stronger me. After all, I climb into bed by myself every night, and how I feel about my actions each day affects me a great deal.

Writing exercise: I will write all the reasons why I like myself and how and why being myself is the best thing I can do.

A SENSE OF COMMUNITY IS IMPORTANT.

My parents made my brothers and me go one night to serve food and baby-sit kids from homeless families. I was very nervous. I thought it would be too sad. But the people were great, and we had fun with the kids. I played cards with the teenage girls and helped hold a little baby.

It did make me sad to think of these kids not having homes of their own. But I was also struck by their ability to enjoy the food, the evening, and to be happy with what they were getting right then. They reminded me to enjoy what I have, to worry less about what I want.

Reaching out to people in need is a good way to remind myself of all I'm grateful for.

READ ALL YOU CAN LAY YOUR HANDS ON,
FROM THE LABEL ON THE KETCHUP BOTTLE TO
LITERATURE'S MASTERS. THE REWARDS OF READING
NEVER DIMINISH AND CONTINUE FOREVER TO BROADEN
YOUR HORIZONS AND BRING PLEASURE TO YOUR LIFE.
–HELEN GANZ

Reading has opened worlds to me. Recently I've been reading a book on Greek mythology that Yolanda lent me. It's an amazing world, and some of its goddesses have been making surprising appearances in my dreams. Reading the newspaper keeps me in touch with what's happening. If I'm having a problem, I can always read about it, and that helps. Reading can make me laugh or cry. It helps me think, imagine, and dream.

Since I was little, people have been telling me how important reading is. But more than ever, I'm realizing that reading helps me be smarter and more spiritually alive. It connects me with people and places all over the globe and all across time.

I treasure reading and will do some today.

LIFE HAS TAUGHT ME ONE SUPREME LESSON.
THAT IS THAT WE MUST—IF WE ARE REALLY TO LIVE AT ALL
—WE MUST PUT OUR CONVICTIONS INTO ACTION.
—MARGARET SANGER

My friend Gita inspires me. If there's something she really cares about, and right now it's environmental issues, she starts writing letters to our congressman and senator. She gets the rest of us to write letters, too. If there's anything going on in school that she thinks should be changed, she's the first to go talk directly to the principal or to start a petition. She's respectful—she just believes it's possible to create change.

I find being around her very hopeful. She thinks our actions matter. Once she wrote an article for the school paper about what we can do as citizens for a better environment—things like not wasting food or water, biking more and driving less, using less paper. She's so passionate that she inspires all of us.

Writing exercise: What are some steps I can take this week to make the world a little better?

TEAMWORK IS IMPORTANT AT HOME AND AT SCHOOL.

Every once in a while my mom says I can't do anything until I clean my room. She and my dad have also set up a schedule for kitchen cleanup and other chores around the house. Sometimes I moan and groan, but really it's not as hard as I like to think it is. And I do always feel good about my room or the kitchen looking better when I'm done.

I can tell that helping out pleases my mom, and she always talks about how my cleaning helps her. My dad notices, too, especially when I'm working in the kitchen. It makes me realize I'm part of a team, and teamwork is an important part of life.

*I need to remember I'm an important part of
the family team, just as I'm a member of my soccer team.
Every little bit of help I give helps our whole family.*

YOU MUST LOVE AND CARE FOR YOURSELF,
BECAUSE THAT'S WHEN THE BEST COMES OUT.
–TINA TURNER

Last Saturday night, instead of being busy and social,
I spent some time with my family. Spending time with
my little brother was actually enjoyable. My mom and I
had a good conversation, and my dad and I had some
good laughs. I took a long bubbly bath and went to bed
early with my book.

It wasn't easy to do this: I hated missing out on fun
with my friends. But I was tired. It felt good to slow down,
be peaceful, and just be home, where we could all let our
hair down. I think the best of me comes out when I take
time like that. An inside strength builds in me.

*I will take time to slow down and love
my life in quiet, peaceful ways.*

PROPERLY FACED, ADVERSITY BUILDS CHARACTER.
–MARY PIPHER

A classmate of ours, Sharee, lost her mother about a year ago. Her dad works and travels a lot and she is on her own a great deal. I didn't know her all that well, but I worried about her, because you could see how sad and lonely she was at first. In fact, I was afraid she'd start going out with the wrong kind of guys just to fight the loneliness.

Instead, she started spending lots of time in the art room: she and the art teacher got pretty close. This week she's got a one-woman show displayed in the halls at school. Some of the paintings have a sad feel to them, and some of them explode with multicolored joy. I ran into her and told her how much I loved her paintings. She lit up. What I couldn't quite say but maybe can one day is how much I admire her courage and her choices.

When things go wrong, I, too, can respond
from the deepest and best part of myself.

BICYCLING HAS DONE MORE TO EMANCIPATE WOMAN
THAN ANY ONE THING IN THE WORLD.... IT GIVES HER
A FEELING OF SELF-RELIANCE AND INDEPENDENCE THE
MOMENT SHE TAKES THE SEAT; AND AWAY SHE GOES,
THE PICTURE OF UNTRAMMELED WOMANHOOD.
–SUSAN B. ANTHONY

Do you remember when you first biked up to your friend's house all by yourself? I felt so liberated to be able to get somewhere pretty fast under my own power! I still feel that way when I get on a bike. Yolanda's mom is a competitive biker and she is so strong and feisty, both on the bike and off.

I like to think of women from way back, hopping on bikes and feeling that sense of freedom, of "untrammeled womanhood." It must be good for the spirit and the soul and the body to ride out in the fresh air and under the open sky. It's better for the air we breathe, too.

When I bike, I'm part of a history of female freedom.
I'm exercising my body and celebrating my soul.

I LOVE MYSELF WHEN I AM LAUGHING. AND THEN
AGAIN WHEN I AM LOOKING MEAN AND IMPRESSIVE.
–ZORA NEALE HURSTON

The woman who wrote this was one of the first black female writers ever published. Imagine how hard that must have been to pull off! It must have taken fierce belief in her own work and self.

When my life seems confusing and complicated, I sometimes think of Zora Neale Hurston. Laughter is important because it connects me to joy. But sometimes life requires me to be tough, to stand up for what I believe in, to not cave in to pressures that would lead me away from what's really important.

When I need to look mean and impressive, I can, and when there's time in my life for laughter and joy, I can enjoy it fully.

WHAT GOD HAS INTENDED FOR YOU GOES
FAR BEYOND ANYTHING YOU CAN IMAGINE.
–OPRAH WINFREY

I like to think that my friends and I have endless pos-
sibilities, both in high school and for the rest of our lives.
Sometimes it's easier for me to believe that about others, but then my friends say they believe the same about
me.

Julia is so good in math and science that she'll place
really high in the state test, and I think she'll be like an
astronaut or an astronomer. Gita is already doing so
much through her church for poor people–she'll end up
doing important work, kind of like Mother Teresa.
When I look at these cool and talented friends of mine,
they remind me that the sky's the limit for all of us.

Imagining a generous and full life will help
me to have one, especially if I let God help me.

I TRY TO EXTRACT SOMETHING POSITIVE FROM
EVERY SITUATION, EVEN IF IT'S JUST LEARNING
NOT TO MAKE THE SAME MISTAKE TWICE.
–CLAUDIA SCHIFFER

My friend Keesha took her parents' car out without asking. Her parents are pretty strict about this. They were at a meeting together, so the other car was home. Keesha wanted to go watch her boyfriend's baseball practice. I tried to talk her out of it; not that many people go watch practices, anyway.

But her boyfriend sometimes talks the sense out of her. I ought to know: the same thing's happened to me. Well, at the ball field someone backed into her car. She had to call home and tell them. It was a mess, and now she's lost driving privileges for a month. The good part is that for the first time, she's talking about how she makes bad choices just for her boyfriend. It's a relief to finally hear her say it. It's a relief that she is actually seeing this in herself.

*Sometimes mistakes help me and my friends
notice behavior in ourselves that needs work and change.
This is the hopeful part of making mistakes.*

HAVING FUN IS SIMPLY HOLDING ON TO THE JOY
OF EACH DAY. IT'S LOOKING UP AT THE SKY AND TAKING
A DEEP BREATH JUST BECAUSE IT FEELS GOOD. . . .
THE JOY OF BEING A KID, AND A GIRL-KID AT THAT,
IS ONE THAT YOU CAN HOLD ON TO FOREVER.
–JUDITH HARLAN

Life can feel so complicated that I desperately need simple, joyful moments. That is one of the reasons I love going to camp. I spend most of the time with other girls, lots of it outside. Looking at the sky and taking time to enjoy it feels great and soothes my soul.

I need to balance more simple joys against the struggles of school: talk, decisions about partying, boyfriends, popularity, coolness. That's one of the reasons I like sports. They offer me the camaraderie of other girls and get me out under the sky.

When life feels confusing or complicated, I can always step outside and cherish the beauty of the sky. It's always there.

> MY EXPERIENCE [AS A PSYCHOLOGIST] IS THAT
> THE MORE MATURE AND HEALTHY GIRLS AVOID SEX . . .
> MOST EARLY SEXUAL ACTIVITY IN OUR CULTURE
> TENDS TO BE HARMFUL TO GIRLS.
> —MARY PIPHER

There are so many messages swirling around about sex. It's cool to be sophisticated and experienced, but how realistic is that? Most girls who are experienced are not respected. I like looking good, and I like kissing my boyfriend, but I want to be strong enough to not get into anything I'm not ready for. Sometimes this makes me nervous. How do I decide what I'm really ready for?

I know from talking to a lot of my friends that this is something we need to think about now, not in the heat of the moment. In grade school we learned ways to say no to peer pressure about using drugs. Maybe we need this in high school for sex: ways to say I can dress sensuously but still say no whenever I want or need to. After all, it's my feelings I wake up with the next morning, and I need to protect myself.

Writing exercise: I will write out at least five ways to say no when I'm feeling uncomfortable with a boy. These can be firm, strong, inventive, or even humorous.

A LOT OF WOMEN SEEM TO THINK THAT
THEY NEED A MAN IN ORDER TO FEEL SECURE
OR TO BE ACCEPTED. I MAY DECIDE I WANT A
BOYFRIEND SOMEDAY, BUT I DON'T NEED ONE.
–LATRICE DAVIS

Some of the girls in my class act like the only thing that makes them important is the guy they're connected to. They put all of their energy into looking good and into catching so-and-so. When I'm tempted to go in that direction, I take a second look. My older cousin, Sheila, has helped me with this. She wishes she had used her talents more in high school and been less focused on boys.

I like boys, but I want my own power. I don't want it to come from who my boyfriend is.

*A strong sense of self will help me wherever
I go in life and whatever I do. It's more important
than whether or not I have a boyfriend.*

ONE OF THE GREAT RICHES I THINK ABOUT [OUR]
MARRIAGE IS [THAT] WE WERE FRIENDS BEFORE WE
BECAME MORE SERIOUS, AND IT'S THAT FRIENDSHIP PLUS
OUR RELATIONSHIP THAT IS AN ENORMOUS STRENGTH.
–MARY ROBINSON

Although I'm not anywhere close to thinking about marriage, I have noticed that dating feels better if I like the guy as a friend. I dated one guy who was really hard to talk to and whose interests were very different from mine. He was interesting and I wanted to get to know him better, but after a while, I realized it was just too hard. Frustrating. I don't think he really wanted to be known any better. When I realized the whole deal was taking but not replenishing a lot of my energy, I broke up with him.

Now I'm with a guy who loves to go skiing with me. We have a lot of mutual friends and do fun things together as a group. It's a blast. I'd have to say the key ingredient here is a sense of friendship.

*When it comes to dating, it helps to balance what
I give with what I get. It helps to be friends.*

ADOLESCENCE IS WHEN GIRLS EXPERIENCE SOCIAL
PRESSURE TO PUT ASIDE THEIR AUTHENTIC SELVES AND
TO DISPLAY ONLY A SMALL PORTION OF THEIR GIFTS.
–MARY PIPHER

Do you ever feel like downplaying one of your talents to fit in? I'm a good writer, and I think I should submit more to the school paper, but I sometimes hold back because I don't want to take any grief for what I've written. Sometimes I hide the fact that I'm genuinely fond of people in my family, because it looks cooler to be mean.

My English teacher strongly encouraged me to publish a story I'd written for his class in the paper. I did, and although I took a tiny bit of teasing, many people told me how much they liked it. That felt great! And since my family will be with me forever while I don't even like some of the "coolest" people in my class, why should I give them so much power.

Sometimes I need the advice of an adult to remind me that it's a lot more important to be who I am than to shrink myself into someone else's definition of coolness.

NOT ONLY CAN WOMEN GET ALONG BEAUTIFULLY,
THERE IS A REAL CAMARADERIE THERE.
–SHERYL CROW

One of the things that I like about being a teenager is getting to just hang out with my friends. We like to go to the mall, and some of us e-mail each other almost every day. I like being around people who know me well. We have a lot of laughs, and I can talk about things that get me down.

But mostly just enjoying each other's company feels good and helps me feel stronger as a person. Friendship adds color to my life and helps hold me up. I know if I really need help, the whole group would be there for me.

I am thankful for all the good friends in my life–
they make it sing!

EVERYONE LIKES TO FEEL GOOD.

My wonderful aunt is recovering from alcoholism and drug use. She says everybody likes to feel good–or another way to put it, everyone likes to feel high. When she quit using, her desire to feel good didn't go away, but she had to find healthy ways to do so. One of the ways she does this is by running. She was always a runner, but during her drug years, she was very inconsistent.

Now, she runs regularly. She says she can count on almost any form of exercise for what she calls an "endorphin high." She says laughter also provides it, and so do a quiet morning in church, a great AA meeting, biking. I realized that some of my sources for feeling high are soccer games, ice skating, laughing on the phone with friends, playing the piano.

Writing exercise: I will write about all the healthy ways I feel good and remember these when I'm tempted to feel good in more risky or illegal ways.

ADVENTURE CAN TAKE MANY FORMS. SOMETIMES,
FOLLOWING YOUR HEART IS THE GREATEST ONE OF ALL.
–DAGNEY SCOTT

I like to think of myself as adventurous and as someone who follows her heart. What does it mean when
these two go together? My friend Angie decided she
wanted to run this huge race in track. Very few girls do
it. She trained hard and went for it despite her parents'
doubts. You should have seen how radiant she was at
the end of that race. She did well, too.

I wrote a book of poems that I finally got the
courage to ask my English teacher to look at. I felt like I
was hanging from my toes at the tip of a skinny branch.
She read the poems, complimented me in great detail,
and suggested ways to improve the poems. The whole
process was scary and incredibly exciting.

*Sometimes following my heart requires
me to be adventurous and courageous.*

AUGUST

IT HAS BEEN SAID THAT GOALS ARE LIKE MAGNETS.
THEY CONSTANTLY PULL US TOWARD THEM.
–JINGER HEATH

Every once in a while I find it important to think about my goals. My goals are to be a good student so I can get into a good college, to be a strong athlete, to continue progressing as a musician. I also want to be a good friend, a good teammate, and a healthy part of my family. When I am too selfish, I work against those last three goals. Then I have to remember the larger picture.

I like the idea of my goals being like a magnet, pulling me. This probably works best when I'm mindful of my goals.

Writing exercise: I will write a list of goals in different areas of my life: self-development, family, friends, education, skills. Then I'll write down what I can do this week to pull myself closer to my goals.

HAVE YOU EVER JUST 'HAD A FEELING' THAT YOU SHOULD
DO SOMETHING? HAVE YOU EVER HAD A PROBLEM AND
'KNOWN' THE ANSWER? THAT'S YOUR INTUITION—
YOUR 'SIXTH SENSE' OR INNER KNOWING.
–CATHERINE DEE

    I have a good friend who lives in Canada, and I only get to talk with her once in a while. But one day last week I kept thinking about her. Couldn't get her off my mind. After school I asked Mom if I could call her, and she said yes. It turns out my friend's dad just lost his job a few days ago, and they were all upset at their house.

    My friend appreciated me calling her so much, and we talked for quite a while about the hard stuff and some fun things going on in both our lives. I know we both felt warmed by the connection. What struck me most was the magic of knowing it was time to call her.

I like to honor that quiet intuitive voice inside me.

HAVE THE COURAGE AND THE DARING
TO THINK THAT YOU CAN MAKE A DIFFERENCE.
THAT'S WHAT BEING YOUNG IS ALL ABOUT.
–RUBY DEE

My family and I volunteered at a shelter for homeless families during Lent before Easter this year. My mom said she really admires the people who coordinate the program. It was a lot of work, but if they didn't do it, more homeless people would be out on the streets. I was struck by the fact that some of these homeless people had children.

I hope we made a difference that night. Maybe when I'm older, I can help in bigger ways. I also help make a difference by being kind and friendly to my elderly neighbors. Sometimes I help the widow next door bring in her groceries. When we bake, Mom always sends me over with a plate of cookies. Gestures like that light up our neighbor's face.

Writing exercise: I will brainstorm ways to make a difference.

CALL IT A CLAN, CALL IT A NETWORK, CALL IT A TRIBE,
CALL IT A FAMILY. WHATEVER YOU CALL IT,
WHOEVER YOU ARE, YOU NEED ONE.
–JANE HOWARD

I was having a rough day yesterday. I was tired and disappointed because we lost our soccer game, and I was goalie for most of the game. I came home, plopped down in a big comfortable chair, and stared out the window. I was feeling crabby, but I just kept quiet. My little brother came up to me and said, "I just love you so much." A little part of me wanted to be mean and push him away, but another part of me melted. It was exactly what I needed to hear.

Sometimes he's the best at reminding me what's most important: that we love and support each other in celebratory times and in quieter, down times. Rather than close my heart, I can open it to this surprising source of comfort.

I will let in the special love of my younger brother.

OH, NEVER MIND THE FASHION. WHEN ONE HAS A STYLE
OF ONE'S OWN, IT IS ALWAYS TWENTY TIMES BETTER.
–MARGARET OLIPHANT

My friends and I have a lot of fun trading makeup
and clothes. Lately we've been into body glitter. One
friend is always doing something wild with her hair. My
friend Lindsay, who is so good at theatre, is in a natural
phase and doesn't believe in shaving. She hikes a lot in
the summertime and really gets into the natural look
then. And it suits her.

In so many ways, teenage years are about expressing
myself and finding ways to know better who I am.
Makeup and clothes are forms of self-expression. I hope
all of us can feel free to try on and see what feels right
and not worry about fitting in.

*Writing exercise: What parts of myself do
I express through my clothes, makeup, and hair?
That's what I want to write about today.*

LOVE IS NOT JUST A TERM FROM THE SIXTIES. IT'S A POWER WE GIVE AND RECEIVE EVERY DAY. . . . LOVE IS A POWER THAT BRINGS POSITIVE ENERGY TO THE BALANCE OF GOOD AND EVIL IN EVERY PERSON AND ELEMENT.
–BOBBI HERVIN

When I feel loving, I have a better day. I usually think of myself as a loving person, but do I show it every day? Unfortunately, no.

Kindness to my friends comes easiest, unless I'm mad at one of them. It's harder for me to show love to my parents and my little brother. It's easier to be generous to my older brother. But when I'm away from my little brother, like when I go to camp, I really do miss him. And his face brightens up and he's so loyal when I'm at all kind to him. It's pretty sweet.

I will look for a place to show my love today,
especially within my family.

CHARACTER IS WHO YOU ARE WHEN NO ONE IS LOOKING.
–KARLA MCGRAY FORSYTH

Lizzie recently got in trouble twice. First she had a car accident, which wouldn't have been so bad except that she was in the opposite part of town from where she told her parents she would be. Then she got caught at a school dance with alcohol on her breath.

Lizzie said that when she complained about getting caught, her minister told her that character was about who she was when no one was looking. That made both of us think twice. Sometimes we focus on what we can get away with, as if that's the important game. But who we are, what our values are, how we treat the people in our lives should be more important than what we can get away with.

If I find myself trying to get away with something, I need to look twice. Am I building my character or weakening it?

I THINK I MAKE A SMIDGEN OF A DIFFERENCE EVERY DAY.
THAT'S MY ULTIMATE GOAL—ON A DAILY BASIS TO MAKE A
DIFFERENCE IN SOMEBODY'S LIFE, EVEN IF IT'S JUST MY OWN.
–LUANA LACY

My mom sent me out to shovel the walk the other day, and while I was out there, I cleared a long strip of the neighbor's sidewalk. She's a widow, and in her seventies. Although she has a snowplow service come, they are often slow, and we know it drives her crazy to have to wait. She waved to me from the window and called later to thank me. She was so appreciative. It made me feel really good.

At Sunday School we talked about doing something like this every day—stepping out of our own thoughts and concerns to do something for somebody else. I have noticed that whenever I do, I feel good.

It's worth making a conscious effort to do something for somebody else every day.

I AM THANKFUL FOR MY FRIENDS BECAUSE
THEY ARE THERE WHEN THE GOOD TIMES AREN'T.
–MARIA BROWN

It often seems like life goes up, then life goes down. Basically I feel like I have a good life, but still there are weeks that are tough or scary. Last month we were afraid my dad had serious heart trouble: he was getting all kinds of tests done. Yolanda and Lizzie helped me get through that by asking every day how I was, how my dad was, and by holding my hand a moment when I first told them.

Dad got a clear bill of health, which made us all happy. I did learn, however, that even when the going gets rough, having my friends around me softens the burden.

Writing exercise: I want to write today about a difficult period I've gone through and how I was helped by reaching out to a friend. Is there anything I'm struggling with today that a friend can help with?

A GOOD FRIEND IS A CONNECTION TO LIFE—
A TIE TO THE PAST, A ROAD TO THE FUTURE,
THE KEY TO SANITY IN A TOTALLY INSANE WORLD.
–LOIS WYSE

I woke up this morning and found e-mails from my good friend at school, Lindsay, and my best out-of-town friend, Alexandra. When I first hopped out of bed I felt a little down, tired maybe. But as soon as I checked my e-mail and found those messages, my heart lifted. I could feel energy pour into me.

I don't know why, but sometimes my friends get my juices flowing. Sometimes the world seems crazy, and the one thing that makes sense is my friends. Or at least they help me to feel that I'm not alone with what's crazy in the world or my home life.

!

*I can honor the importance of my friends
by being a considerate friend myself.*

SPIRITUAL ROLE MODELS ARE IMPORTANT.

My friend Jessica belongs to a synagogue, and the female rabbi there seems very cool. Jessica is always telling me something her rabbi said in a sermon or to her individually that either comforted her or made her think. This rabbi is full of life: she's smart, funny, and outspoken.

My cousin sings in the church choir, and her choir director is really cool. She's just a petite woman, but you should see her conduct this huge choir! There's nothing small about her power when she's conducting. I only know these women a little bit, but I look up to them, and sometimes I think, now how would the rabbi respond to this? What would the choir director think of that?

*Being around people who are clear
about their spiritual path can help me.*

WOMEN'S PROPENSITY TO SHARE CONFIDENCES IS
UNIVERSAL. WE CONFIRM OUR REALITY BY SHARING.
–BARBARA GRIZZUTI HARRISON

I remember being on the playground in fifth grade and talking about my cousin who had just been hospitalized for a drug overdose. He used to be one of my favorite cousins. I started to cry, and the next thing I knew, five of my friends were all around me. Jenny, whose dad is a minister, did an impromptu prayer service.

I felt incredibly comforted. Before talking, I had felt totally distracted, almost stuck inside my thoughts and worries. But after talking, I felt better, like I could keep moving forward, because of the concern of my friends.

Almost anything is bearable, I think,
with friends around to help me.

IT'S ALWAYS MORE MEANINGFUL AND WONDERFUL WHEN
YOU CAN SHARE YOUR LIFE AND GOALS WITH OTHERS.
GREAT FRIENDS AND FAMILY ARE KEY.
–MISSY GIOVE

I have an older cousin who just published her first book. It was a novel. She told me that it was so gratifying that her close friends and family knew how hard she had worked for years before she got published. And these people kept telling her how much she deserved the honor. Whereas someone who didn't know her well might have thought such an accomplishment came easily.

Another older cousin of mine told me about watching her best friend act in a play in New York. She said seeing how good Michelle was made her cry from happiness.

The friendships of my life include this kind of caring. They're important parts of anything I accomplish now or later.

IF YOU'RE NEVER SCARED OR EMBARRASSED OR HURT,
IT MEANS YOU NEVER TAKE ANY CHANCES.
–JULIA SOREL

I decided to try out for the girls softball team this year. The first night of practice, I was embarrassed: I couldn't bat, and I missed every ball I reached for. But I hadn't played since the previous spring. I was tempted to give up after this, but I didn't, and my skills improved each night. The actual tryouts came the following week, and I made the team! But first I had to go through the discomfort of being rusty and clumsy.

Whenever I try something new, self-consciousness goes with the experience. Sometimes I feel embarrassed, but other times I feel scared. I'm learning that taking chances makes life more fun and interesting. It's worth going through the initial discomfort. Reminding myself about this helps me talk myself through the rough periods.

It takes courage to challenge myself and to keep walking through self-consciousness. It's always worth it.

IT IS THIS BELIEF IN A POWER LARGER THAN MYSELF AND
OTHER THAN MYSELF WHICH ALLOWS ME TO VENTURE
INTO THE UNKNOWN AND EVEN THE UNKNOWABLE.
–MAYA ANGELOU

My uncle was telling me that a cornerstone of his Alcoholics Anonymous program is belief in a Higher Power. He was telling me about Step 2: "Came to believe that a power greater than ourselves could restore us to sanity." Most of the steps talk about getting help and guidance and sustenance from this higher power. Other people find comfort other places. My mom has been taking us to church lately, where the readings and homilies are all about God as a source of comfort and strength. A friend at school tells me about the ceremonies on her grandmother's reservation, and how her grandmother talks daily about the Great Spirit.

*Writing exercise: I will write about this power in my life,
this power which is larger than myself. How do I envision it?
Where do I see it working in my life?*

HEED THE STILL, SMALL VOICE THAT SO SELDOM
LEADS US WRONG AND NEVER INTO FOLLY.
–MARQUISE DU DEFFAND

Last spring my friend Brittany, who I don't know very well, invited me to a party at her house. She didn't tell me very much about it, and I got a funny feeling right away. Later, I heard two boys talking about how her parents were gone and they were going to crash it. The way they talked made me feel weird, too, and they aren't my favorite guys in the school.

I was flattered to be asked and kind of curious, but all day that Friday something felt funny about the whole deal. So I ended up telling Brittany I couldn't come. It wasn't an easy thing to do, but I felt relieved afterward. On Monday the talk of the school was how Brittany's party got busted by police and everybody who was there and drinking really got in trouble, especially the athletes.

I am thankful for the quiet voice inside me.
It's there to help me. All I have to do is listen.

CAN YOU IMAGINE WHAT WOULD HAPPEN
IF GIRLS TOOK ALL THE ENERGY THEY SPEND
WORRYING ABOUT THEIR IMAGE AND PUT IT INTO
PAINTING, WRITING, THEORIZING, SCIENCE OR SPORTS?
–JOAN JACOBS BRUMBERG

A common trap for me, kind of like a rut in a well-used road, is to spend way too much time worrying about how I look. Some of my friends are even worse. We go through different phases with it. Angie has been driving me nuts this month. She has a crush on David, and all she could talk about was how her makeup looked or about her new pants. Boring! And she's so brilliant and talented. It made me sad and mad. If David is a good guy, he's going to like her for a lot more than just how she looks.

Anyway, I love the idea that all this energy can be put into painting or writing or science. It's a lot of energy; I know that. We're a lot more interesting when our energy is going places other than how we look.

Today I will give my looks only a passing thought
and put my energy into the world or into my creativity.

IT'S IMPORTANT TO FOLLOW YOUR WISHING HEART.
–LISA LOBE

Wishes begin in the heart. I think there are different levels of them. There's the surface level of wishing for things (clothes, a new CD). Then there's the deeper level of wishing for happier relationships with friends or family. Wishes are often about our talents and dreams. Wishing to learn to sing well enough to solo in the choir, wishing to play piano well enough to play a certain difficult sonata, wishing to find a way to paint well and be recognized for it.

Wishes come in many forms, but they connect directly to our hearts. It's good to follow these wishes, especially the deeper ones.

Writing exercise: I will write at least a page or two of lines that begin with the words, "I wish..."
Then I will write about steps I can take toward those wishes.

SOMETIMES IT TAKES A VISITOR FROM A DIFFERENT
WORLD TO HELP ME SEE WHAT I HAVE.

The other day my dad took me to buy tickets for a
rock concert. We had to stand in line for about ten minutes before it was our turn to get in the door. This ticket
window is downtown. While we stood there, traffic
went by steadily, both cars and people on foot.

An older man caught our attention. He was singing
and walking slowly, but his clothes were dirty, and when
I looked closer at him, I could see that most of his teeth
were missing. He was friendly, smiling and talking to us,
but he didn't smell very good. After he walked away, my
dad told me he was probably homeless and had no
place to shower or clean up.

All day I thought about him: I felt sad for him, but I
kept remembering his smile. All day I appreciated having a home, a shower, clean clothes, and a dad who
takes care of me.

*Writing exercise: I will think about all the things
I am fortunate to have. Either I'll make a long list
or I'll write about one or two of them in detail.*

TROUBLE IS A PART OF YOUR LIFE, AND IF YOU DON'T
SHARE IT, YOU DON'T GIVE THE PERSON WHO LOVES
YOU ENOUGH CHANCE TO LOVE YOU ENOUGH.
–DINAH SHORE

The other night Mom and I had a big argument–she
said no to something I really wanted to do. I went off to
my room and slammed my door. When the phone rang,
it was for me. I told Mom I wasn't talking to anybody and
to go away. I wanted to hang onto my anger, to clutch it
like a pillow. But after a while I got bored. I called my
friend back and told her about the argument.

Before long she had me laughing and was telling me
stories about her arguments with her mom. Sometimes I
think everybody else has a perfect relationship with her
mom and I'm the only one who struggles. But when I
actually reach out and talk about something that troubles me, I find out I'm not alone. People all around me
care about me–if I let them.

Instead of hanging onto something I'm mad about,
I will share it with a friend, a parent, or my journal.

PAY ATTENTION TO KINDNESSES IN THIS WORLD.

My mom and I were at the grocery store when she saw an elderly neighbor of ours sitting next to a row of grocery bags. Mom went up and asked her if she needed a ride home. Doris's eyes lit up. She asked my mom if she was sure that would be okay. "I'd be happy to give you a ride," Mom said. So, Doris canceled her cab, and we loaded her six bags of groceries next to ours and drove Doris home.

She didn't want us to come inside, but she let us carry her bags up to the door. She thanked us so much. When we drove on, I told my mom that was kind of her, and I could tell she liked hearing that. I felt proud of her for taking the time to notice and offer the ride to our neighbor. And I felt proud to have been part of it all.

*I will take time to notice kindness in others
and to be a force for kindness myself.*

THE MORE THE SOUL KNOWS, THE MORE SHE
LOVES AND LOVING MUCH, SHE TASTES MUCH.
–ST. CATHERINE OF SIENA

People have different ideas about what the soul is. Is it the breath of life, a soft breeze that blows through everything we feel or see? Is it the part of us that is most spiritual? Is it the part of us that connects to a larger force, perhaps called the universe or God or the Great Spirit?

St. Catherine's thoughts on the soul point out the soul's connection to love. The more we know of this world, the more we can love it. To know a tree well is to love it. To know a garden well, through planting and weeding, is to love it deeply. To go through hard and joyful times with friends and family is to know and love them more. When someone says, "She's got a lot of soul," don't they mean that she has a lot of life and spirit and love that spills out of her?

Writing exercise: I will imagine my soul.

I FIND . . .
IN ALL POOR FOOLISH THINGS THAT LIVE A DAY,
ETERNAL BEAUTY WANDERING ON HER WAY.
–WILLIAM BUTLER YEATS

My favorite thing at our cabin is watching the sunset every night. We cheer on the changing colors, the indigo and rose of the clouds, the way everything is reflected across the water. Just noticing the sunset calms us all down and excites us, I think, even if we're eating or clearing the table at the same time.

Sometimes my mom stops the car to watch the moon come up, or she has me look closely at and smell a peony she has just picked from the garden. When I take the time, I breathe those luscious scents and notice the layers of petals, the incredible richness of the colors.

Such moments are often fleeting, but they bring a special, hopeful, and uplifting feeling to me.

Writing exercise: I will describe in detail
a moment today when I noticed something.

WITHIN YOU THERE IS A STILLNESS AND A SANCTUARY TO
WHICH YOU CAN RETREAT AT ANYTIME AND BE YOURSELF.
–HERMANN HESSE

Sometimes I feel like my moods take me places I don't want to go; they swing me high and swing me low. I get out of kilter just because one friend is talking to someone else more than to me. Or I'm jealous of how one friend looks or has done on her test or because she seems to have a better social life than I do. Any of these things can pull me off center, and I start to look outside of myself for answers, and of course there are no answers there.

If something bothers me, I need to look inside. If I find myself trying to please others too much, I need to get quiet and see what feels right for me. Sometimes the phrase Be Yourself is harder than it sounds, and sometimes it's easier than I expect. But it can't happen without taking the time to look inside and listen quietly, alone.

*I will take some quiet time for thinking and
soul searching. This always helps me be myself.*

Loss can shape me in surprising ways.

I have a friend, Lizzie, whose older brother has done lots of drugs. I know this makes Lizzie really sad, and she only talks about him once in a while. She told me that in her Sunday School class, she made a prayer flag for him. When we wrote goals for ourselves in language arts, one of her goals was to not waste her life like her brother has. One time she told me that it's very weird because it's like she doesn't have a brother, and yet she does have one. He would rather be off using his drugs than having anything to do with normal family time.

Lizzie is one of my best friends–she is passionate about life and about using her brains and talents. She's a lot of fun. I sometimes think this sadness in her life, which gets her down from time to time, also nourishes her awareness of how precious life and loved ones are.

Writing exercise: I will write about a loss I have suffered in my life. After writing about my sadness and disappointment, I will also write about what I have learned from this loss.

THERE'S MORE TO ME THAN MEETS THE EYE.

You'd think from looking at the cover of most teen and women's magazines that to be beautiful means to be really thin and to have a certain kind of face and smile. I sometimes fall into believing that, and then I start to notice everything wrong with my body. My waist isn't small enough, I don't like my hair, my thighs are too big.

My Aunt Jane gets really tough with me about this. She insists that beauty comes in all sizes. According to her, this media hype about how we should look is dangerous because it's limiting and superficial. She always reminds me that beauty is what shines from deep within us. It's easy for me to see her beauty–it's in her warmth, her feistiness, and her smile.

I will pay attention to all the things I like about my body just as it is. I will honor the self inside–that's what's most important.

WE HAVE ALL BEEN CREATED FOR GREAT THINGS—
TO LOVE AND BE LOVED. . . . LOVE IN ACTION
IS WHAT GIVES US GRACE.
–MOTHER TERESA

Mother Teresa is woman who has inspired me. I saw a program on TV about her. Here she was, this tiny, weathered woman, holding a dying man in her arms. She moved large numbers of people, including me, to care for the poor and the hungry. And she always seemed to value the spiritual worth of the people she helped: she was always learning from them.

She was born on this day, August 27th, in 1910. When she died, the whole world mourned and honored her. Because of her, I signed up to volunteer at the local food shelf. Shaiwan, Creona, Cassie, and I work together one Saturday morning each month. It gives me a glimmer of what Mother Teresa meant when she said love in action gives us grace.

When I reach out to help others,
a sense of grace flows into me.

FAMILY IS LIKE THE FOUNDATION OF A HOUSE AND
FRIENDS ARE THE FURNISHINGS. BOTH ARE IMPORTANT.

My feelings about my family these days remind me
of a yo-yo or a seesaw. First I want to push my mother
away, and then I desperately need her, maybe just to
drive me somewhere. I alternate between being crazy
about my dad and then being driven crazy by him. I
want to wring my little brother's neck, and a moment
later I feel the urge to give him a big hug, because
nobody loves me like he does.

The truth is, nobody loves me like my mom and dad.
Every summer we take a long car trip. I always fight
with my brothers. Last year I missed the trip because I
was at camp. And you know what? I felt so sad about
missing it that we arranged our summer plans so we
could all go together this year.

*Family meals and family outings help keep me
connected to my parents and brothers, who are still
important to me, even though I want to push them away.*

STONES ARE CALLED GRANDFATHERS AND GRANDMOTHERS
AND ARE EXTREMELY IMPORTANT IN OJIBWE PHILOSOPHY.
ONCE I BEGAN TO THINK OF STONES AS ANIMATE,
I STARTED TO WONDER WHETHER I WAS PICKING UP A
STONE OR IT WAS PUTTING ITSELF IN MY HANDS.
–LOUISE ERDRICH

Everywhere I go, I collect rocks and stones. For that matter, so does everyone in my family. We come back from our summer vacation with our own collections. My parents like to collect large stones to use in our yard. There are window ledges and shelves in our home decorated with stones.

It amazes me how certain rocks attract me, how they almost jump out at me. Amazing. Mysterious. Magical. If Ojibwe tradition believes stones are alive, then perhaps they have secrets or wisdom to impart if I listen. I love the feel of my stones: they often calm or enliven me.

Writing exercise: I will take one of my favorite rocks, hold it in my hand, and describe it. Then I will ask it questions and see what it has to say to me.

PEOPLE THINK THAT WHEN SOMETHING
'GOES WRONG' IT'S THEIR FAULT. IF ONLY THEY
HAD DONE SOMETHING DIFFERENTLY. BUT SOMETIMES
THINGS GO WRONG TO TEACH YOU WHAT IS RIGHT.
–ALICE WALKER

Have you ever felt things going wrong? It happens to me in different ways. Something doesn't turn out the way I wanted it to, like my birthday party, for instance. I invited too many girls, including two I didn't know all that well. They went off and did their own thing at the party, and it bothered everybody else, including me. Looking back, I wasn't very smart to invite so many, especially girls I'm not really close to.

Other times I just have a bad day and things go wrong. I need to remember that I don't have to feel at fault on top of struggling with whatever's gone wrong. Instead, I can look for the lesson, for what the experience has to teach me.

The next time I feel things are going wrong, I can skip blaming myself and go right to the lesson I'm supposed to learn.

HOWEVER YOU DECORATE YOUR BODY,
ENJOY YOURSELF . . . DON'T TAKE IT TOO SERIOUSLY.
YOUR BODY IS BEAUTIFUL, WITHOUT ALL THE BAUBLES
AND BANGLES AND BOWS. SO HAVE FUN. . . .
–CARMEN RENEE BERRY

When I go to camp, I don't wear makeup for days. I'm camping, canoeing, and swimming all the time. I like being free of makeup and not worrying about my hair. I notice how good we all look with nothing but old clothes and sunshine and fresh air on our skin. Camp always gives me strength when I get too concerned about how I look.

When I'm back in school, it is fun to wear sparkles and some lipstick. Sometimes I experiment with other kinds of makeup and jewelry. It is fun, as long as I remember that how I look is just part of who I am. I don't need to wear makeup to feel okay about myself. I can choose to wear it or go without.

Decorating my body is fun, especially when it's done to express myself and not to meet anybody else's expectations.

SEPTEMBER

ONE OF THE HARDEST HABITS TO QUIT IS SMOKING.
AND IT'S AN EASY ONE TO SLIP INTO.

Did you recently see someone you know light up a cigarette at a party? Did it look sort of cool? Well, I tried it once and almost choked. Lately I have been listening to people talk about this. My dad says it's the hardest thing in the world to quit once you're hooked, and it's way too easy to get hooked. My cousin has a friend who is trying to quit, and it's so hard that sometimes she cries about it.

Sports helps me with this issue. I've read enough to know what smoking would do to my skating and running. And it helps that a lot of other people won't smoke because of athletics and because they're into having healthy, active bodies. It may look cool for a second, but it's not cool to have stale cigarette breath or the smell on your clothes or the stain on your teeth and in your lungs. Cool is placing at the state track meet or publishing a poem.

*Writing exercise: How does being cool sometimes fool me?
What is it that really seems cool to me?*

THE PROCESS OF LIFE, FROM YOUTH TO
MIDDLE AGE TO OLD AGE TO DEATH, IS TO
CREATE SOMETHING BEAUTIFUL—THE SOUL.
–AI JA LEE

I sometimes wonder about my soul. What it is, where does it reside in my body? I've heard people say the soul leaves the body soon after death. That makes me think the soul has wings.

I have always thought of my grandmother as having a beautiful soul. Her eyes are deep and clear and gentle and fierce all at the same time. She has passions: painting, reading, walking, gardening, music. She still plays the piano and walks every day. And she's never pushy with her affection, but she loves me in ways I'm comfortable being loved. I think my grandmother feeds her soul regularly, and that's why it's so beautiful.

What can I do today to feed my soul? I can do something I love, like pick a bouquet of flowers.

LABOR DAY FLOATS, BUT IT'S ALWAYS ABOUT NOW.

Labor Day weekend marks the end of summer and the beginning of the school year. In a lot of ways, it marks the opening of a new phase of work. I play more in the summer. There are fewer demands on my time and I recreate-re-create-in many ways.

But now comes the time to set goals for the year ahead and to have one last summer celebration. It's a sort of bittersweet celebration. I'm sad to see the end of carefree summer, even though I look forward to school.

Writing exercise: I will write about some ways this summer was special and about my goals for this school year.

IT'S HIGH TIME THERE WAS A 'GRRRLS' CLUB' WHERE
WE STUCK TOGETHER NO MATTER WHAT. IF WE'RE
FIGHTING EACH OTHER CONSTANTLY, WE'LL ALL LOSE,
BUT IF WE'RE ALL IN IT TOGETHER, WHO KNOWS
WHAT AMAZING THINGS WE'LL ACCOMPLISH?
–MINDY MORGENSTERN

When I was a little younger, my friends and I fought more. We argued, ganged up on one another, left one person out one day and another the next. Thank goodness we seem to be growing out of that! What a waste of energy. It was so hurtful, too.

I think we're realizing that together, helping and supporting each other, we're a lot stronger. When Shaiwan's mom died, it brought us all together. We helped babysit her little brother and brought over food our mothers made. Our parents all pitched in and helped out, too.

*Girls unite!!! We go better and faster
when we're cheering each other on.*

BEGINNINGS ARE IMPORTANT.

The beginning of the school year is exciting! Besides new clothes and new school supplies, there's the rush of seeing everybody again. During summer we get fragmented, but school brings everybody back together again.

Beginnings are a time to think about what I want in the year ahead, both academically and personally. Friends, grades, activities. I like to take time to think about them all.

Writing exercise: I will spend time every night this first week of school writing about my goals and dreams for the year ahead.

CELEBRATE YOUR FEET BY DANCING ON YOUR TOES,
YOUR TONGUE BY CATCHING SUMMER RAINDROPS,
AND YOUR SKIN BY LETTING SOMEONE HUG YOU.
–CARMEN RENEE BERRY

I alternate between being too focused on my body and ignoring it. I'm sure there's a happy medium. Lately I've been ignoring my body. But for my birthday I got new bath salts and lotion. And tonight I took a long bath and then spread lotion slowly over my body. My skin felt soft and tingly all over. Then when my mom came in to say good night, I asked her for a hug. That felt good, too.

The whole evening made me realize it has been a long time since I had treated my body to some special nurturing. It feels so good. So does dancing–anywhere, anytime. So does catching rain or snowdrops on my tongue.

*My body deserves scented lotion, dancing feet,
and rain and snow kisses on a regular basis.*

ON THE SURFACE, USING [DRUGS AND ALCOHOL]
MAY SEEM LIKE A WAY TO CALM YOUR FEAR AND BELONG.
BUT IN REALITY, ALCOHOL AND DRUG USE CAN
MAKE GROWING UP EVEN HARDER.
–GLADYS FOLKERS AND JEANNE ENGELMANN

My teenage years seem turbulent. There are so many ups and downs! I feel like I've gone from an innocent little girl to a fully developed young woman in such a short time. My mood swings seem connected to my monthly cycle, and I don't have any control over that. I used to want my mom at all my games at school, and now I don't. And then there's boys and that whole world.

My dad says it's easy to grab onto alcohol or drugs for a few moments of confidence or escape because of all these changes. Some kids end up wanting the drugs more than the confidence they thought the drugs would give them.

I can find healthy ways to make it through the ups and downs. These will build my confidence and prepare me for the future.

SOMEONE HAS SAID THAT THE GREATEST CAUSE OF
ULCERS IS MOUNTAIN-CLIMBING OVER MOLEHILLS.
–MAXWELL MALTZ

Ulcers happen in the stomach. Although I'm too young to have them, I have noticed how if I'm upset, I often feel it first in my stomach. It's no accident that after seeing something horrible, people often throw up. Our relationship to food and digestion seems connected to what we're feeling.

I've been trying to write to my stomach when it feels weird. Having a dialogue with my stomach sounds weird, I know, but it has helped me. I've discovered that worry enters my stomach and gives me cramps. If I hand over my worry to my God or Great Spirit or angels, my body feels healthier and lighter.

*Writing exercise: The next time I get a stomachache,
I will write a dialogue between me and my stomach.
Maybe we can learn to work together.*

> TRUSTING OUR INTUITION OFTEN
> SAVES US FROM DISASTER.
> –ANNE WILSON SCHAEF

My mom took me to a self-defense workshop last week. We learned some simple moves and strategies for when we feel threatened. One of the things that struck me was the importance of intuition and paying attention. The workshop leader told several stories about women escaping danger because something or someone felt wrong or because the women felt just slightly uneasy. These women reacted intuitively and honored their feelings enough to act immediately.

My intuition is a blend of feelings in my heart and my body. All I need to do is feel the tightness in my chest when I see a stranger's face. Feel and then take action.

My intuition is a good friend. I need to pay attention to her.

THERE ARE LOTS OF WAYS TO BE A SMALL
BUT IMPORTANT PART OF A GREATER WHOLE.

One of the ways I have earned money is baby-sitting. Sometimes I feel I'm getting too busy to do much of it, but when I do, it's fun. I get to be a kid again by playing with the kids. And I enjoy having younger children admire me. I have a favorite family I baby-sit for, and those kids make me Christmas cards and let me know how much they like me. That feels good!

Their family went through a rough time a few months ago. Their mother was hospitalized for two weeks. I helped out because the kids are comfortable with me. I brought some fun into that scary time of their lives. I know how much the parents appreciated it: they told me over and over.

Baby-sitting can be an important contribution to my neighborhood and community. And it can be fun!

IF YOU'RE WORRIED ABOUT A FRIEND WHO MIGHT
HAVE AN EATING DISORDER, TALK TO HER AND TO
AN ADULT WHO CAN OFFER HELP AND GUIDANCE.
–GLADYS FOLKERS AND JEANNE ENGELMANN

At first my friends and I made jokes about how Cassie wouldn't eat a pea without worrying about gaining weight. But one day I noticed how skinny her arms were. I saw that she never ate anything. She passed out in gym class one day, and now she's dropped out of many of the activities she used to participate in.

So one day I gathered my courage and wrote her a note. I told her what a great friend she's been, and how I miss the old sparkly Cassie, and how she looks too thin. I told her I was concerned and if she wanted to talk about it, I was ready to listen. Then I went and talked to the school counselor. The school counselor called a session with Cassie and her parents, and now she is getting help for her anorexia. And she's talking to me again.

Sometimes the more serious problems among my friends require the involvement of a trusted adult. Let me always do what is best for my friends, even when it isn't easy.

IT IS JUST AN OLD HABIT. HABITS DIE HARD.
BUT THEY DIE CERTAINLY—IF ONE PERSISTS, THEY DIE.
—MA DEVA PADMA

My bad habit is chewing my nails. I never used to do it. But I've been nervous lately, I think because I'm doing something new. I'm in the school play, and I worry about learning my lines, about talking loud enough on stage. So instead of talking about my nervousness or writing it down I've been chewing my nails.

My mom says habits can be broken with persistence and effort. My dad used to smoke, and he dropped that habit: he said it was very hard at first, but after a while it became much easier. Every day that I don't chew my nails, I reward myself somehow.

*A key to changing old behaviors is
to not get discouraged. If I have a bad day,
I'll keep at it and reward myself for good days.*

THE HARVEST MOON FESTIVAL IS CELEBRATED ON FALL'S FIRST FULL MOON.

This is an Asian celebration in honor of the moon. When the moon is full, people gather to thank it for bountiful harvests. Moon cakes are a special part of the meal and the celebration: they are round like the moon and sweet. Sometimes families try to capture the moon's reflection in a large bowl of water.

Full moons always feel special to me, even more so if I'm near water and can see the moon's reflection. The full moon in fall represents the end of summer crops and the beginning of a new season.

Writing exercise: I will celebrate the full moon by writing about its light shining across our yard through the leaves of my favorite tree and into my room.

> HIS GOOD LOOKS AND POPULARITY
> HAD MADE HIM SO INORDINATELY CONCEITED
> THAT THEY BLINDED HIM TO . . . POSSIBILITY.
> –MAYA ANGELOU

Popularity is fleeting, fickle, yet seductive. We all want to be popular. But my dad always tells me to watch out for popularity. Sometimes it is a superficial road. Instead, he says, build good, solid friendships. Develop qualities that will nourish healthy relationships all my life long.

If my focus becomes popularity, I may behave in ways that will win other people's approval, instead of in ways I believe in and that feel right to me. The other day I saw the popular kids heading down the hall, laughing and talking, and then I saw my quiet friend at her locker, looking sort of sad. I went over to her instead of making the popular choice. I was glad I did, because she really needed to talk.

Sometimes friendship means not being at center stage but in the wings, reaching out to someone else.

Is there tension between your shoulder blades?
Fifteen minutes of stretching and breathing
exercises may be just what you need.
–Carmen Renee Berry

We had two exams today, and I stayed up late last night at the computer lab finishing a huge paper. By the time I came home, my shoulders ached. Only I didn't realize it until my mom started rubbing them. Then I could feel the pain in those muscles, the ache of long hours of work.

School can be stressful. Too often there's a lot due at one time. It's good in a way that I'm so challenged, but if my body reacts, I need to work out the stress. Exercise helps a lot, and so does sleep. Just sitting still and concentrating on breathing can drain tension from my body. If I stretch my arms and back and legs, I feel more relaxed and energized. Even five minutes of massage can do wonders!

*I need to pay attention to where stress collects
in my body and find ways to release it.*

IT'S IMPORTANT TO LEARN TO DEAL WITH YOUR
MOOD SWINGS AND FEELINGS IN A POSITIVE WAY.
RATHER THAN REACHING FOR DRUGS OR ALCOHOL,
TRY COMFORTING YOURSELF IN HEALTHY WAYS:
TAKE A HOT BATH, CALL A FRIEND, TAKE A WALK,
DO YOGA, DRAW, OR BUY YOURSELF SOME FLOWERS.
–GLADYS FOLKERS AND JEANNE ENGELMANN

My cousin went through treatment for drugs and alcohol. She told me she started drinking when she was about 14. Her parents were getting divorced and she felt lonely. She hooked up with an older boy, and he was really into partying. Before long that had become her favorite way to comfort herself and to let her hair down. The drinking dragged her down so fast: her grades dropped, she lost good friends, and she began to drop all of her other interests.

The sad part is, she feels like she wasted years of her life. Now she's 24, and she is learning all the other, healthier ways to cope with life's problems. She doesn't want me to make the same mistake.

Writing exercise: What comforts me? A hot scented bath, talking by phone or e-mail to a good friend, a long bike ride. I will write down what comforts me in healthy ways.

I'VE LEARNED TO TAKE TIME FOR MYSELF AND TO TREAT
MYSELF WITH A GREAT LOVE AND A GREAT DEAL OF
RESPECT 'CAUSE I LIKE ME. . . . I THINK I'M KIND OF COOL.
–WHOOPI GOLDBERG

What does treating myself with a great deal of love
and respect mean? Part of it is paying attention to feelings in my body. If I feel tired, I deserve to go to bed
early and get some extra rest. Or if I'm hungry, I deserve
to eat healthy food so I feel good.

Part of self-respect is realizing I don't need to be
around people who mistreat me; I deserve to be around
people who like me as I am. If a situation feels off to me,
I can honor my body's feeling by figuring out what I
need to do.

I

*It's important to love and respect others,
but I have to love and respect myself first.*

I BELIEVE THE MOST IMPORTANT THING IS NOT TO
LOSE THE PERSPECTIVE OF WHERE ONE IS HEADING.
–BENAZIR BHUTTO

Every summer my family takes a road trip. I love reading the map and figuring out how far our next destination is. We go on a long trip, so we stop a lot along the way. We enjoy the scenery, we stop to eat and sometimes to swim. But we always know where we're headed and the map helps us to see where we're going and how far we've come.

I like to post my dreams and goals on the wall of my room as a map of where I'm headed. Journal writing is like a road map, too, because I can look back at where I've come from. Having goals helps me: I want to be on the Honor Roll, learn Moonlight Sonata on the piano by memory, get grades good enough to get into any college I want, and more.

!

*Writing exercise: I will draw a road map of my dreams
and goals and post them on my bedroom wall.*

YOU'VE GOT TO MAKE YOUR OWN KIND OF MUSIC
SING YOUR OWN SPECIAL SONG
MAKE YOUR OWN KIND OF MUSIC
EVEN IF NOBODY ELSE SINGS ALONG.
–MAMA CASS

The other day my friends and I had a great conversation. Each of us talked about how she feels different in some way. Often we're self-conscious about our differences, but our talk seemed to change that. Lindsay feels self-conscious because she's heavy, but that never bothers the rest of us, and we told her so. Shaiwan worries about being not quite smart enough, but we think she's the wittiest and funniest member of our group.

Creona is always organizing volunteer work in the community, and she said she worries that people groan when they see her coming. We told her how much we admire what she does and how we've learned from it. Our conversation made me realize that everybody feels alone some of the time.

I want to remember that singing my own song is what's important, both when I'm singing alone and when I'm singing harmony.

I KNEW THAT JUDAISM HAD YOM KIPPUR,
THE DAY OF ATONEMENT, WHEN WE FASTED
AND ASKED FOR FORGIVENESS FOR THE THINGS
WE'D DONE WRONG IN THE COURSE OF THE YEAR.
–RUTH BRIN

For Jews, Rosh Hashanah begins the New Year and the ten days of putting life in order for Yom Kippur. These are the High Holy Days for Judaism, and the dates change every year, based on the lunar calendar. But always around this time, Jewish people look at their lives and make amends, asking for forgiveness where it is needed.

I like the idea of having a time of year regularly set aside for this kind of reflection and soul searching. On Rosh Hashanah, apples are dipped in honey to symbolize the hope that the year ahead will be a sweet one. Rebecca tells me about all these things, and I love it. I like to borrow a little from all the religions I learn about.

*From Judaism I can learn the value of
regularly looking at my life and, where I need to,
making amends or asking forgiveness.*

FALL EQUINOX MARKS THE END OF
SUMMER AND THE BEGINNING OF FALL.

This time of year, I feel so much change in the air. I can smell autumn leaves and hear them crunch beneath my feet. I'm sad about saying good-bye to summer's special freedoms: I will miss swimming in lakes and going on picnics and riding bikes on warm, hazy, lazy days.

But the gold and orange leaves outside my window seem to say, autumn blazes with its own treats! I'm happy to see old friends and favorite teachers again. I even enjoy settling into the routine of reading and studying more. And I love the smells of fall—the leaves, the earth after a pounding autumn rain.

*Writing exercise: I will describe what I love about
fall and what I'd like to learn in the months to come.*

MANY GIRLS HAVE THE WRONG IDEA ABOUT
HOW THEY SHOULD—OR EVEN CAN—LOOK.
DIETING, STARVING, OR BINGEING AND PURGING CAN
OVER TIME MAKE SOMEONE LOOK A LOT WORSE.
–GLADYS FOLKERS AND JEANNE ENGELMANN

From time to time I fall into the trap of thinking I need to diet. What I have learned from experience and from watching other people is that weight loss from diet rarely lasts very long. My aunt went to Weight Watchers, a program that focuses on balanced eating, not starving. Three meals a day, lots of fruits and vegetables, and lots of water. My aunt slowly lost weight and has been eating that way ever since. She looks great.

My mom is sort of a health nut. There are always lots of fruits and vegetables and whole-grain breads in the house. But I have a weakness for sugar and am sometimes rebellious about it. My body knows when I'm eating well and drinking a lot of water. I have more energy. Exercise helps keep me in shape and feels good, too.

*I look and feel my best when I eat healthy,
exercise, sleep well, and take care of my soul.*

EVERYTHING'S NOT ABOUT WINNING IN THE
CLASSICAL SENSE. THE KEY IS LEARNING TO ENJOY
THE PROCESS ALONG THE WAY. BECAUSE MOST TIMES
YOU'LL LEARN SOMETHING NEW ABOUT YOURSELF IN
THE PROCESS AND THAT, MY FRIENDS, IS WINNING.
–MINDY MORGENSTERN

I wanted to win first place in the track meet. but I
got a side ache halfway through my run, and it slowed
me down. I was able to finish, though, so I learned that I
could push myself in spite of pain. But I also learned to
honor the limits of my body. If I had pushed harder, I
might not have crossed the finish line.

When Creona passed me, I felt crushed at first. Then
I thought, better that she win than someone from the
other team! And when I crossed the line, she was waiting for me. I congratulated her, and she was worried
about me. It was a good trade.

*Every experience, even the ones that are
hard to take, can teach me an important lesson.*

> IF MY YOUNGER SISTER TOLD ME SHE WANTED TO SMOKE,
> I'D TELL HER, 'IT'LL BE THE WORST MISTAKE
> YOU'LL EVER MAKE. DON'T DO IT.'
> —MARIA

We just finished a unit in health class on smoking. It was an eye-opener. One thing that struck me is the power of the media in promoting this national pastime. For instance, six years after the Virginia Slims ads were introduced, twice as many teenage girls were smoking. Why are we so easily manipulated? It's to nobody's benefit but the tobacco companies' bank accounts.

A thousand Americans die every day from smoking-related diseases. Smoking stains teeth and causes bad breath and bad-smelling clothes. In spite of all this bad news, there's still something alluring about the cigarette at the end of one's fingers. But my friends and I are sure we can find better-smelling and healthier routes to sophistication.

I don't want to get started on a habit that a lot of people have a really hard time walking away from.

THE BODY IS LIKE A RIVER OF INFORMATION AND ENERGY,
WE ARE LEARNING, AND ALL ITS PARTS HAVE A DYNAMIC
COMMUNICATION WITH ALL THE OTHER PARTS.
–CHRISTIANE NORTHRUP, M.D.

If my toes get pinched into shoes that don't fit right,
they throw my hips off. If I'm dressed too warm for the
day, I feel sluggish. If I'm cold, I shiver and tense up all
over. If I've been eating too much sugar, my stomach
feels unsettled and my energy surges and then crashes.

I like to think of all the parts of my body as tributaries to the main river. What I feed and how I exercise my
body affect every part of me. How I rest my body
affects every organ and limb, not to mention my heart
and soul and energy level.

*Writing exercise: what am I doing to take care of my body's
needs? Writing it down will help me be more conscious.*

NEVER UNDERESTIMATE THE POWER OF A KIND WORD OR DEED.

My friend Jenny is known for being kind. She smiles easily at everyone and seems to mean it. If someone is going through a hard time, she is the first to know what to do or say.

When my dad's dad died, several neighbors brought food over. It was so kind of them and helped soften the shock and sadness of Grandpa's death. I had a hard week last week and had mentioned to my mom that I would love some of my favorite muffins for Saturday morning breakfast. Then I forgot I had said that until Saturday morning, when I woke up smelling that wonderful blueberry muffin smell.

*Practicing and receiving kindness
will remind me of its power.*

WE INHERIT FROM OUR ANCESTORS GIFTS
SO OFTEN TAKEN FOR GRANTED—OUR NAMES,
THE COLOR OF OUR EYES AND THE TEXTURE OF
OUR HAIR, THE UNFOLDING OF VARIED ABILITIES
AND INTEREST IN DIFFERENT SUBJECTS. . . .
WE ARE LINKS BETWEEN THE AGES, CONTAINING . . .
SACRED MEMORIES AND FUTURE PROMISE.
–EDWARD C. SELLNOR

Every once in a while, I think about what I've inherited. My cousin says I look a lot like my dad. My brother and I have similar features. We've got my dad's long fingers and legs. When I look at my face, I see my mom's deep brown eyes. Shaiwan was adopted, but she seemed to have inherited her adoptive mother's love for dance.

When I see a gift's been passed down to me, it makes me want to nurture it. Perhaps I can pass on my grandmother's love of singing through my own voice and someday through my own children.

Let me notice and nurture all I have inherited.

TAKE A MUSIC-BATH ONCE OR TWICE A WEEK FOR A FEW
SEASONS, AND YOU WILL FIND THAT IT IS TO THE SOUL
WHAT THE WATER-BATH IS TO THE BODY.
–OLIVER WENDELL HOLMES

I'm crazy about baths. They always relax me and
make me feel better, no matter how I felt when I first
slipped my foot into the water. Lately I've noticed that
if I listen to my classical music tape, I get the same kind
of feeling in my body. The violins and other instruments
relax and uplift me.

Listening to rock and roll, good jazz, and the blues
affects my body, too, but in different ways. They energize me, juice me up, make me feel like moving.

*I can let music bathe, energize,
or calm me whenever I need to.*

EVERY FAMILY IS FREAKY IN ITS OWN UNIQUE WAY.
–MINDY MORGENSTERN

Do you ever feel like your family is weird or wrong? My dad is so embarrassing when he is crabby. When he is in a good mood, everyone loves him, but I don't like my friends to see him when he's crabby. And my little brother has been known to "toot," as he calls it (also known as passing gas), when my friends are with us in the car. Totally embarrassing.

When I'm having a rough day, it's easy to believe everybody else has a perfect family. Sometimes I think my family is like a bag with torn seams; what is untidy about us spills out. I'm beginning to think that's human nature–every family has stuff that breaks through the neat seams.

Nobody's perfect–no person, no family. Even in the midst of imperfections, though, we can want the best for each other.

THE POWER OF STORYTELLING LIES IN ITS EMBODIED TRUTH. . . . THEIR BODIES REMEMBER WHAT IT IS LIKE TO A BE A NOBODY AND WHAT IT IS LIKE TO BE SOMEBODY.
–CHUNG HYUN KYUNG

One thing I have noticed about my mom and dad is that, every day, they trade stories of their day. Sometimes my dad rattles away and my mom is quieter, but there is always some exchange. My mom always asks how my day was, but I don't often volunteer too much. Then some days I'm in the mood to talk, and out it comes. And it feels good. It's true–it makes me feel like I'm somebody when I have someone listen to my day.

Besides the day's smaller stories, occasional big stories come up. Like when my cousin had the bad car accident and ended up in the hospital. I felt like I was living in a tunnel until I told my friends about that.

If I have a story to tell today,
I'll tell it instead of keeping it inside.

OCTOBER

> THE HANDS ARE ONE OF THE MOST COMPLEX
> STRUCTURES IN OUR BODY . . . THEY ARE EXQUISITELY
> SENSITIVE AND LOVE BEING MASSAGED.
> –ROBERT THE

Last night I had worked for hours on a research paper and was tired and crabby. When my mom came in to say good night, she sat on the edge of my bed and massaged my hands. They were sore from typing so much, and it felt great. My mom and I have been struggling with each other, and it was good to not talk. I felt so loved.

I'm going to do the same for my mom some time in the next couple of days. Maybe I can even get my friends to take turns massaging each other's hands. Our hands do so much, that it's a treat for them to be touched and pampered.

*I can trade a hand massage with someone I love
and it will be a healing, energizing treat–for free.*

Do you have something in your life that makes you feel like a failure? We all do. So, join the club. When the little voice nags at you, nag back.
–Carmen Renee Berry

Sometimes I speak up and say things I probably shouldn't. Then I get in trouble. Then I say to myself, There I go again, too stupid to know when I should just button it up. When it comes to my loose tongue, I come down on myself about as hard as Jenny does for not being able to carry a tune or as Gita does for not being very athletic. We can all be pretty hard on ourselves.

But I can drown out my failure voice, sometimes by shouting it down. Or I paste up messages on my mirror and walls that remind me to accept and celebrate myself. My favorites: "I am exactly where I need to be right now" and "I rock!" These help me when I read them every day.

If the bad voice speaks up,
I can drown it out with good voices.

NOTHING IS MORE MEMORABLE THAN A SCENT.
–DIANE ACKERMAN

My friends and I are crazy about scented body and bath lotions. My favorite scent is Kiwi-Grapefruit, and it feels so luxurious to spread the lotion all over me and then breathe it in. I also love to immerse myself in a scented bath. It's relaxing and pleasant in a simple way. I always feel better afterward.

Another favorite smell is the smell of my mom's coffee cake baking or just out of the oven. I know it's going to be a great day when I smell that. Wonderful smells create warm memories.

!

Writing exercise: I'll write a list of my favorite smells. How can I make smells give me more pleasure today?

LIKE DRINKING AND DRIVING, DRINKING
AND SEX MAKE A RISKY COMBINATION, TOO.

My dad handed me an article the other day on date rape. I didn't want to read it, but it talked a lot about girls and women who ended up getting raped or almost raped by a date. I had never heard of it before, but the article quoted several teenagers and older women, so I knew it had to be real.

No matter what, rape is rape and these girls and women were the victims. In some cases, though, the girl had so much to drink she made poor decisions all along the way. Like going to someone's hotel room. Like leaving her friends and their dates. Like hanging out at unchaperoned parties with older boys there. This information added a whole other layer to the drug and alcohol issue for me.

Every step of the way I need to make clear and healthy choices for my heart, soul, and body. They are all connected.

WHY HARP ON OLD MISTAKES THAT WE REGRET?
WHY BE A RAINY DAY?

It's easy to hang onto old mistakes, both my own and other people's. I'm especially good at holding onto mistakes my parents or my brothers make. Days or weeks later, I'm still bringing it up. But I'm hard on myself, too.

I'd like to be more like the snakes I track in the summertime. When a snake is done with its skin, it rubs against a rock or tree, slides out the opening, and leaves it behind. Leaves it behind! It's called molting. I'd like to work on molting the skin of old mistakes. While they're still around me, they make it hard to breathe.

*When I feel myself in the grip of one of
my old mistakes, or someone else's, I can choose
to work it free, let it go, and leave it behind.*

SPIRIT IS INVISIBLE TO THE BODY'S EYES
AND CANNOT BE HEARD WITH EARS ALONE,
AND YET SOUNDS AND OBJECTS BEGIN TO BRIGHTEN
AS I FOCUS ON MY SPIRITUAL SIGHT.
–HUGH PRATHER

It's true that when my spirits are up, I look at the world in a much brighter and more focused way. My mom always says that eyes are the windows to the soul. Clear eyes in a person appeal to her. And to tell the truth, they do to me, too. When I see people who drink or smoke dope a lot, their eyes seem cloudy. That's the first thing I notice.

Not using chemicals is one way to focus on my spiritual sight. Having a place to go to worship helps, too–the synagogue, the church, the meditation room all exude a sense of spiritual life. Being near water and trees makes my spirit feel alive. And helping other people does, too.

Writing exercise: What are the ways I feed my spirit?
How does this affect what I see?

> YOUR FIRST BOYFRIEND SHOULD BE LIKE THE
> FIRST PANCAKE. JUST A TESTER TO SEE IF THE
> GRIDDLE IS HOT ENOUGH.
> –MINDY MORGENSTERN

This saying makes me laugh. It's so funny. But I also think it's true. The first guy I went to the movies with was fun and a nice guy, but we didn't last very long. I think we both were interested in getting to know other people, too. Also, he and I have very different interests.

It's not a pretty sight when a girl or guy wants to hang onto that first special person. The hanging on can look so desperate. We're at the age when it's more fun to get to know other people and not just focus on one so much.

Going out with boys is a process of testing out myself and the experience. It's important to be respectful, but there's no need to hang on when it's time to move on.

> HOW BEAUTIFUL, HOW GRAND
> AND LIBERATING THIS EXPERIENCE IS,
> WHEN PEOPLE LEARN TO HELP EACH OTHER.
> –DR. PAUL TOURNIER

My friend Creona and I have been writing notes, letters, and e-mails to each other for a couple of weeks. She is having a rough time with her stepmother. At first she was happy when her dad remarried, because she doesn't see that much of her mom. But her stepmom takes over too much she's too bossy and she keeps telling Creona's dad that she'll take care of everything. But Creona wants her dad to take care of most things connected to her.

I've been going through a hard time with my friend Lindsay. All she cares about right now is her boyfriend. And I miss her. So Creona and I are keeping each other's head above water. We're in very few classes together, but through our notes and e-mail we stay close.

It seems that no matter what problem I am struggling with, there is always at least one person I can talk it over with. This is a beautiful and liberating thing.

WE ARE ALL IMPORTANT BRANCHES ON THE TREE OF LIFE.

Shaiwan got us all to sign up for this tutoring program. One day a week we go help elementary school kids who are having trouble with math or reading. We work one-to-one in the halls of the school. This has become a favorite part of my week. I work with a little boy named Tyrone, and his face lights up when he sees me. We read books, and I help him sound out words and letters, and I can see that he's improved over the months. This feels so good, because I know nothing will help him as much in life as becoming a good reader.

Shaiwan is always good at helping me and my friends look at the bigger picture. She is passionate about us being part of a larger community, in our city and in our world. When I step out of the box of my small daily concerns, I realize there's a lot I can contribute to the larger picture.

What am I doing to contribute to this world?

> BUT THERE'S SOMETHING TERRIBLY IMPORTANT
> YOU NEED TO KNOW ABOUT THIS NATIONAL
> FIXATION WITH BEING THIN: IT'S A SHAM. . . .
> BARBIE ISN'T THE REAL THING. SHE'S PLASTIC.
> –GLADYS FOLKERS AND JEANNE ENGELMANN

I have to say that when I think about how we all think we're supposed to look like Barbie, it makes me want to scream. It really makes me angry. It's easy to say that of course we don't expect to look like the doll. But almost every model we see in magazines or on TV or in the movies looks suspiciously like Barbie.

So. We are being bombarded by this image of plastic–this image that's impossible to attain or retain without starving and seriously compromising our health. It's stupid, really, yet we're all susceptible to it. And we're all hurt by it.

Writing exercise: What are some of the ways the perfect body icon has hurt me or my friends? I'll create three body affirmations that specifically tell me how much I love my body. Then I'll post them on my wall.

ASK QUESTIONS.
EXPAND YOUR HORIZONS BY RAISING YOUR HAND.
–MINDY MORGENSTERN

We had a special instructor in theater yesterday and today. Yesterday I had a very quiet, shy-feeling day. When I felt a question inside of me, I swallowed it. But today I let my hand go up. In spite of some fear that my question might sound really stupid, I blurted it out. The instructor said it was a good question, and her answer was really interesting. She seemed cool, so I stayed after class and talked with her alone for a few minutes.

I ended up being so glad I had raised my hand. My curiosity opened a new door for me: I'm glad I listened to and expressed that curiosity.

*I can open up my own world by asking
questions when my heart wants and needs to.*

IF YOU KNOW THAT YOU GET OVERLY SENSITIVE AROUND
THE TIME OF YOUR PERIOD, TRY TO KEEP THAT IN MIND.
–KAREN AND JENNIFER GRAVELLE

The other day I felt more crabby than usual, for no
good reason that I could really see. I was very short-
tempered with my mom and little brother. Shaiwan said
something to me on the phone that reduced me to
tears, and Shaiwan couldn't figure out why and neither
could I.

Then my period arrived, and I remembered that
sometimes right before my period my emotions ride the
roller-coaster. If I keep track of my cycle, it helps me to
calm down and breathe deep and not overreact to people. Some of my other friends have a similar experience,
although Shaiwan doesn't seem bothered by any changes
in her monthly cycle.

*Knowledge is power. The more I know
about my body, the better I can protect myself
and cope with my moods and hormone swings.*

TO LIGHT A CANDLE BY MYSELF IS
ONE OF MY FAVORITE PRAYERS.
–BROTHER DAVID STEINDL-RAST

Prayer is something I'm not always good at or comfortable with. My grandmother is the best pray-er I know. She is always sending me prayer cards. If she knows we're struggling with something here at our house, she says, "I'll say a prayer for you." And I know she genuinely means it.

I like the idea of being alone with a candle flame as a form of prayer. There is something reflective and reverent about the spark of the match, then the moment the flame ignites, like a torch being passed on. The steady beauty of the small flame lights up the darkness around it.

!

If there is something in my life that can use prayer, I will light a candle and reflect while it lights up the darkness in its special serene way.

VISUAL ART HOLDS IMMENSE POTENTIAL
FOR HEALING AND INSPIRATION.

I remember my mother gave me a coloring book when I was in first grade. It was full of art masterpieces, waiting for me to color them in. I'm taking an art class right now, and we study a couple of painters and then try to paint in their style.

Picasso's "The Old Guitarist" is my favorite one right now. The old man reminds me of my grandfather, who is sick and losing weight. There's such an air of sadness and yet beauty to the shades of blue and the figure in the painting. Even my friend Yolanda, who isn't that interested in art, could see what I meant: she felt it too.

Paintings can be a source of expression in my life.
I can always pick up an art book or go to a museum,
and I will be touched in some way.

THERE IS NO SINGLE PERFECT BODY IMAGE
OR TYPE. EVERY BODY IS AS UNIQUE AND
SPECIAL AS THE PERSON WHO INHABITS IT.
–GLADYS FOLKERS AND JEANNE ENGELMANN

My mom made me go to a workshop on the female body. But she let me bring some of my friends. What I thought would be a pretty dorky day was actually great. Not only did we all learn a lot, but we also felt special in new ways about being female.

We talked about how all of us can find things wrong with our bodies. Lindsay thinks her hips are too big. I think my stomach isn't flat enough. Shaiwan wishes she had longer legs. The entire last half of the day we talked about what our bodies do for us, and what we love about them. I love my hair, my legs, which run fast in soccer and on the field, and the way my body can move gracefully across the ice.

Writing exercise: Every time I notice what is wrong with my body, I will write five things I love about my body or things I'm grateful it can do.

GUYS WILL COME AND GUYS WILL GO,
BUT MOST FRIENDS ARE FOREVER.
–MINDY MORGENSTERN

Sometimes guys interfere with friendships. I've seen it happen with my friends when they both like the same guy. I saw Jessica do whatever she could to "win" this guy–even purposely leaving out her good friend Shaiwan a lot of the time. Jessica and this guy only hung out with each other for about a month, then he went on to someone else. It took Jessica many months to repair her friendship with Shaiwan.

My female friends are important to me. I hope I never fall hard for the same guy as my best friend, but if I do, I hope I am kinder, more considerate, and more aware of the long-range picture than Jessica was.

In the balance between boys and good friends,
the value of friendship holds a lot of weight.

HE'LL TAKE ALL THE MUSIC OUT OF YOU.
–LANGSTON HUGHES

I think it's important to pay attention to who or what takes the music out of me and who helps keep the music alive inside me. I dated a boy for a while who is so cute and so popular. But he isn't very nice. He found all sorts of ways to put me down. I'd come away puzzled and hurt and confused. Here, so many girls wanted him and I had him, but it didn't feel good. What's wrong with me, I wondered, that it doesn't feel good?

I talked about it with my older brother's girlfriend, of all people. She really seemed to understand and told me I deserved to feel happier. So I broke up with him. He took too much of the music out of my soul.

It helps to listen to the singing inside of me. If someone around me is muffling my song, I can say good-bye.

WHEN I AM PARTICULARLY WORN DOWN BY A DAY,
I CAN BE TOTALLY REJUVENATED BY SLEEP.

Every once in a while I have an anxious day. I'm afraid my friends don't like me as much as they used to. I'm afraid the fight my mom and dad had means the end of our family life. I'm afraid I didn't do as well on my math test as I should have. I'm afraid I'll never be able to please my mom and dad.

When I'm feeling particularly left out and fearful for no real reason, I need to look at my overall energy level. If I have been too busy and am tired, it's so easy to see only life's dark side. It's so easy to think, "I can't do that. It won't work. Nothing is going right." Shakespeare once wrote, "Sleep . . . knits up the raveled sleeve of care."

*If I feel anxious and lonely, a good night's sleep
can heal me and return me to a brighter view of life.*

FOLLOW YOUR HEART, LOVE WILL FIND YOU,
TRUTH WILL UNBIND YOU,
SING OUT A SONG OF THE SOUL.
–CRIS WILLIAMSON

My heart feels free when I'm singing. It comes alive when I'm laughing with a friend or really listening to her. It sings when I'm doing well in school, when I'm flying down a ski hill on a sunny winter day, and when I'm helping other people.

I like to be around people who help my heart sing, who get behind my passions. I love the idea that if I pursue what I really care about, love will come find me and the truth of my loves will free me. Free me to sing–every day–the song of my soul.

Writing exercise: over the next few days, I will write in detail about all the things that make my heart sing. What does it mean to me, right now in my life, to follow my heart?

> WITH EVENING'S COMING, THE FLOWER
> FOLDS HER PETALS AND SLEEPS, EMBRACING
> HER LONGING. AT MORNING'S APPROACH SHE
> OPENS HER LIPS TO MEET THE SUN'S KISS.
> –KAHLIL GIBRAN

There's a woman at our church who is a spiritual advisor. She has studied theology and prayer for years and helps people with the spiritual part of their lives. She's become good friends with my mom, and once in a while I go to talks that she gives. Recently she talked about longing, and how it's part of the human condition. Deep inside most longings, she believes, is the desire to connect with our deepest spiritual selves, with God.

It helped to hear this and to think about it. And it helps to think of the flower embracing her longing as she curls into sleep. At times, when I feel myself longing for what at the moment I do not have, I can hold the longing close and curl into the healing power of sleep. And then I can wake up again, ready to taste all that life has to offer me, right now.

Longing is part of the human condition. It is as beautiful as flowers, as much a part of any spiritual journey as prayer is.

THE MORE YOU LEARN ABOUT WHAT TO EXPECT AS YOUR BODY GOES THROUGH ITS OWN MENSTRUAL CYCLE, THE EASIER IT WILL BE TO HANDLE HAVING YOUR PERIOD.
–KAREN AND JENNIFER GRAVELLE

When you get your period, it's like joining a club–the womanhood club. No boys allowed. Some girls start their periods early; others quite late. Some have cramps and pain, and others hardly notice anything. Some of us are regular as clockwork, while others have sporadic periods. Some of my friends feel emotionally out-of-whack for a few days before their periods show up; others struggle more with the actual bleeding itself.

In this club, everyone's experience is different, yet what my friends and I have in common is that we all have something to cope with, to figure out. It helps to talk with each other and with our moms. We trade tips, like never wear white pants on a heavy day. And it helps to laugh about stuff like that, like the embarrassing possibility of bleeding through, which we all worry about.

Being female is like being a member of an exclusive club. It's helpful to talk club strategies and coping skills once in a while.

LEARN TO MEDITATE. IT CLEARS YOUR MIND, CALMS
YOU DOWN AND HELPS YOU TO KNOW THE TRUTH.
–MINDY MORGENSTERN

My aunt taught me a way to meditate that's pretty easy. She told me to just close my eyes and first of all relax my body, all the way from my head to my feet. Then she said to breathe deep, several times, breathe in warmth and light, and breathe out any worries. By the time I did these things, I was already feeling much more relaxed and slowed down–light and floaty as a feather.

Then she had me imagine myself in my favorite place in the world. It could be an imaginary spot or somewhere I've been. I imagined the blue water and sand beach and rocky shore of our cabin. I felt peaceful and beautiful inside.

*Anytime I want to, I can close my eyes and travel
to a place of peace and serenity and beauty.*

I READ IN THE HOPE OF DISCOVERING THE TRUTH,
OR AT LEAST SOME TRUTHS. . . . I SEEK CLUES THAT
MIGHT EXPLAIN LIFE'S ODDITIES, THAT MIGHT LIGHT
UP THE DARK CORNERS OF EXISTENCE A LITTLE,
THAT MIGHT MAKE MY OWN STAY HERE ON EARTH
MORE INTERESTING, IF NOT MORE PLEASANT.
–JOSEPH EPSTEIN

Lots of kids my age wonder what is the truth of our own lives, our parents' lives, and life in general. I'm struggling with questions like: Does organized religion really help? And how do I know there is a God? There are adults in my life who can direct me to books to help me think about these things. My parents are pretty good librarians, and so is my favorite English teacher.

I read books to help me wrestle with important questions, and I read them to find out about many things in this world. I also read for the pleasure of getting to know characters and going on adventures with them.

May the right book help me with what I most need this week. All I need to do is browse at the library or ask the right person to find it.

EVERYONE NEEDS A SPIRITUAL GUIDE. . . .
MY OWN WISE FRIEND IS MY DOG. HE MAKES
FRIENDS EASILY AND DOESN'T HOLD A GRUDGE.
-GARY KOWALSKI

We have two cats at my house; they came to us when they were kittens. It struck me the other day, and I even said this to my mom, that I'm always telling the cats I love them, but that I hardly tell her I love her. It was an eye-opening realization for me.

The cats seem to bring out a tender part of me. No matter how I am feeling about myself, I always feel loved by them. It's easy to be genuinely affectionate toward them. Maybe once in a while I could give that same kind of genuine, easy affection to my little brother or my mother. I wonder if the cats can teach me how to be a more loving person.

In appreciation of the unconditional love
I receive and give to my pets, I can learn
to be more that way with family members.

PART OF THE FEAST IS BECOMING AWARE OF THE
WORLD THAT IS MINE. PART OF THE FEAST IS OWNING
THIS BROKEN WORLD AS MY OWN BROKENNESS.
–MACRINA WIEDERKEHR

Sometimes the stuff that goes on in the world that
we hear on the news or read about in the paper is so
depressing. One of the things that has really gotten to
me and my friends is all the school shootings. It's scary
because we all know students who are into guns and
violent talk.

It seems important to pay attention to what is going
on in the world at large and in the world around me.
Maybe if someone had paid closer attention along the
way, one or more of those shootings could have been
prevented. At any rate, it's my world. It's our world. And
we need to find ways to live through even the most difficult things.

My friends, my family, and my belief in a kind and loving
force greater than us humans can help me keep my boat
afloat in spite of this broken world's stormy waters.

THE PIE IS RELIGIOUS, SOMETHING FROM GOD.
THE ONLY PART OF THE MEAL TO BE EATEN SLOWLY.
HUGE PIECES, A QUARTER PIE PER PERSON, AND
BETWEEN EACH BITE, A DRINK OF COFFEE . . .
–GARY PAULSEN

Today is National Pie Day. Now, this is a rather
wacky and quirky part of our culture, I think, to have
something as silly as National Pie Day. Still, it's fun.

In my family, pie holds a certain fond place. When
we go to our cabin in the summertime, we eat pie often.
There's a bakery in the nearby small town that makes
the best pies. It's our favorite time of year in some ways,
because we're all relaxed and just there to slow down
and have fun. But all year we dream about those rasp-
berry-rhubarb pies, warm and fresh out of the oven.
And every summer, we feel like the luckiest people on
earth when we return and slice into the first piece.

*Writing exercise: What are some of the
favorite foods my family and I share?
What special memories are tied to these foods?*

WAKING INTO THE NEW DAY, WE ARE
ALL OF US ADAM ON THE MORNING OF
CREATION, AND THE WORLD IS OURS TO NAME.
–FREDERICK BUECHNER

The world is ours to name. On a Sunday morning, I might name the day a day to relax, to see more of my family than I usually do. Monday, I might name as one for getting back to my projects, to the things hanging over my head that I know I need to do. Wednesday is the day I play soccer this week, so I get to see all my favorite friends and run until my body feels both incredibly alive and incredibly sore.

I like the idea of each morning presenting an open slate on which I get to write. When I look at each day from the sleepy haze of my bedroom, surrounded by my favorite posters, snuggled under my soft comforter, I can find something special to look forward to each day.

Naming my day is a good thing to do every morning, almost like a way of being thankful for the day ahead.

IF YOU LOOK DEEPLY INTO THE PALM OF
YOUR HAND, YOU WILL SEE YOUR PARENTS AND
ALL GENERATIONS OF YOUR ANCESTORS. . . . YOU ARE
THE CONTINUATION OF EACH OF THESE PEOPLE.
–THICH NHAT HANH

Hands are like road maps, physical geography of the generations and of our own uniqueness. When I look at mine I can see my father's wrinkles and my mother's long fingers: piano hands, her father calls her hands. When I think about Grandma and Grandpa on both sides, I think of how hard those hands worked. How much they wanted to pass on a better life to their children and children's children.

It makes me wonder if I'm appreciating the gifts they worked so hard to pass on. This is worth thinking about, for some of my favorite people in the world are my grandparents.

Writing exercise: I'd like to describe my own hands and then the hands of my parents and grandparents. What lessons, what roadways open to me in the lines across my palms?

HOLD FAST TO DREAMS
FOR IF DREAMS DIE,
LIFE IS A BROKEN-WINGED BIRD
THAT CANNOT FLY.
–LANGSTON HUGHES

My friends and I sometimes talk about our dreams, short term and long term. Jobs we want to get next year and jobs we want to be doing when we're 25. Accomplishments, honors we want to achieve. I want to keep skating and maybe skate professionally, but I also want to be a lawyer. Lindsay wants to become a concert pianist, and Shaiwan wants to continue with her dancing and become a member of a modern dance company.

Gita wants to work with poor people and help set up programs for them to help themselves. I can see where each of my friends' dreams fit them. It helps to pay attention to dreams, to see the connection between what I do every day and my dreams for my life.

Dreams, large and small ones, give my life wings.

LET YOUR GIFTS SHINE. POLISH THEM.

My dad says that in his experience as a teacher, he sees adolescent girls sometimes hiding how smart they are in order to fit in. I can see this sometimes, yet the girls I admire the most are the ones who don't hold back at all. They are out there with their brains and talent. People sometimes resent really smart girls, but what's the point in hiding brains? I think intelligence is always admired, even if the admiration happens secretly.

Dad also says that we have a spiritual obligation to develop whatever brains and skills we were born with. It really would be a shame to hide or waste them.

Am I polishing my talents and brains? Let me have enough courage to celebrate and not hide who I am.

HALLOWEEN, OR ALL HALLOW'S EVE, HAS BEEN
CELEBRATED IN SOME WAY FOR CENTURIES.

Before I went out to join my friends for a Halloween
party, the little five-year-old from next door came to
our house. I baby-sit him sometimes, and I knew he was
scared about Halloween. All the witches and ghosts up
all over had been scaring him for weeks. When I looked
at his mother quizzically, she shrugged her shoulders as
if to say, "I can't explain it." She looked so happy. He was
happy. "Trick or treat," he said, beaming up at me.

I told him he looked great, and I gave him his
favorite treat—a grape lollipop—and he skipped as he
went on his way. And I thought how these old customs
still continue to bring people together, in simple and
festive ways.

*Writing exercise: Before I go to bed tonight, I will
write about the moment with that little boy and
any other impressions of this special evening.*

November

THE WORLD BREAKS EVERYONE AND AFTERWARD
MANY ARE STRONG AT THE BROKEN PLACES.
–ERNEST HEMINGWAY

I have two friends, Cassie and Creona, whose parents are divorcing. They are so sad their moms and dads are breaking up. Both say it's been coming for a long time. Cassie's parents always led very separate lives, and Creona's parents always fought a lot. Still, the actual deal of having two places to live, and having their parents living in separate places has been rough.

My cousin went through this with her parents, and she's almost 30 now. She says she learned a lot about friendship and healing and that she needs to be very wise in her choice of a marriage partner. She can see things now that she learned from the heartbreak, and in many ways she is stronger because of what she has been through. I'm hoping Cassie and Creona do the same.

I can help strengthen broken hearts around me by being a good friend. My turn to be the one in need will come.

THE LOVE OF OUR NEIGHBOR IN ALL ITS FULLNESS
SIMPLY MEANS BEING ABLE TO SAY
"WHAT ARE YOU GOING THROUGH?"
–SIMONE WEIL

I think of myself as a loving person. But I don't think I ask the people in my life how they are doing often enough. It's easy to forget to do when I'm so busy. I know when someone asks me and then really listens, it means everything to me.

The other day I asked my brother how he was doing, and I think he was shocked. But he sat down and talked to me as if I were his equal for a whole five minutes. It felt great. This encouraged me to try it on my mom: she almost burst into tears, she was so touched. She says that is what she and her friends do for each other all the time.

I will ask someone I care about how she is doing today.

TO LOVE AT ALL IS TO BE VULNERABLE.
–C.S. LEWIS

Okay . . . I think I'm going through my first heart-break. I've watched it happen to my friends, when the person they like doesn't like them anymore. For a few weeks I had so much fun with Tyler that I just wanted it to keep going. Then it seemed like he pulled back and was distant. Now I've seen him walking and talking with Alison a lot. And I heard a rumor he's going to ask her to the big dance coming up.

I find I cry easily, and it's hard to get my energy up for anything. My friend Lindsay, who went through it a couple months ago, tells me it will pass. She already feels fine again. And her comforting shoulder has helped me through this a lot. I guess part of the risk of reaching out on the limb of love is of breaking my heart.

All broken hearts heal, especially with
kindness from friends and family.

BEDTIME IS A GOOD TIME TO REVIEW THE DAY.

I have started writing in my journal at night. My uncle is a minister, and he says that he encourages everyone to take time to reflect back on the day. He especially encourages paying attention to any behavior we want to change and noticing the small gifts and good things that came our way.

I have noticed that by writing at bedtime, I remember things I might otherwise forget. For example, I remember that I need to pay special attention to Teresa tomorrow because she's going through a rough period in her family, and I practically ignored her all of one day. I also remember that my band teacher said to drop in and I forgot to. I also remember that my mom made my favorite cookies, which she hasn't done in ages. I wonder what inspired her? I didn't have time to ask.

*Writing exercise: Each night for the next week,
I am going to reflect on my day in my journal.*

THE WORLD OF BIRDS IS COLORFUL AND MAGICAL.

Our science teacher made us go birding one day with a friend of hers who studies birds. We saw an oriole, whose chest is a brilliant orange. We saw many cardinals—their bright red shouting out to us in the midst of green leaves. I paid attention to the deep blue of the blue jays in a way I never had before. Such an incredible and deep shade of blue! And the best one was the indigo bunting. Very difficult to spot, he said. It was our lucky day, and that shade of bluish lavender melted all of us. After it flew away, we ooh'ed and aah'ed.

There are so many worlds within our world. I never would have thought twice before about birds. But spending the day with this bird lover taught me a lot. There's beauty and magic in these smaller worlds, waiting for me to notice.

My life is richer and more colorful, the more of the varied worlds around me that I take in.

MUSIC WEAVES JOY.

I have noticed lately how much all music affects me, not just my favorite songs on the radio. My dad took me to a classical concert the other night, and one of the songs almost made me cry. Then a flute solo came along and I wanted to get up and dance. When I walked out of the concert hall, I felt strangely energized and peaceful.

It's made me think that I could use music more often. It can soothe me or settle me down one day. It can rev me up, maybe even get me dancing, another. My dad gave me some classical music on tape: listening to it at night is supposed to help you do well on tests the next day.

Music of all kinds can help calm me or pick me up.
Whatever I need, there's music for my soul.

WOMEN FOUGHT LONG AND HARD
TO EARN THE RIGHT TO VOTE.

I did a paper for history class on Susan B. Anthony. She did so much to earn women the right to vote. And of course she took a lot of heat for it, often from the women around her. She was ahead of her time, because today none of us can imagine this country as a place where women aren't allowed to vote.

I think it must have been lonely for Susan B. Anthony. I admire her fierce beliefs, her ability to find other women to work with on this cause, and her ability to keep her eyes on the prize, in spite of being very unpopular in some circles.

*Writing exercise: I will write about the women
who have paved the way for me to have a better life:
women of history and women in my family.*

THERE IS NOTHING MORE FRAGILE THAN
A SNOWFLAKE, BUT LOOK AT WHAT THEY
CAN DO WHEN THEY BOND TOGETHER.

Enough snowflakes piled together can stop the world: cars can't drive, buses get stuck. Blizzards and avalanches bring the lives within them to a halt. Yet there is nothing more delicate than an individual snowflake. It doesn't last in the warmth of my hand for longer than a minute. Each one is unique, beautiful, and airy as lace.

I often feel fragile myself. And I realize over and over again how much my friends and family make me strong. It's the support of others who want the best for me that helps keep me strong and forceful.

*When I'm feeling fragile, I can always reach out
for a warm hug to bond with someone who loves me.*

BE COURAGEOUS ENOUGH TO GROW
INTO THE FLOWER YOU WERE MEANT TO BE.

A seed sometimes has to fight its way into blossom. Think of flowers that grow out of granite rock, flowers that survive heavy rains and winds before blossoming into beautiful shapes and colors.

Sometimes being a smart or talented girl means people don't want me to bloom as fully as I can. Some try to cloud me over with criticism or rain on me with thinly disguised jealousy or blow breezes of resentment in my direction. It all hurts, and sometimes it's tempting to fold in on myself to make them more comfortable. But really, why should I? Like each flower, aren't I meant to offer the world all the talents and skills I have?

Writing exercise: What are some of the ways I need courage in my life right now, in order to blossom fully?

E-MAIL IS THE LATEST FORM OF LETTER WRITING.

I am so grateful for e-mail. My friends and I have a whole new way to connect with and ask advice from each other. Plus I'm able to have an ongoing conversation with my grandmother. That's great, because I usually only see her twice a year.

I have smoothed out disagreements with both of my parents on e-mail, and figured out solutions. No one could interrupt each other. My dad and mom each took time out from their workday to communicate and come up with a compromise we could all live with.

E-mail, electronic as it is, can provide healing and emotional interactions between me and my loved ones.

VETERAN'S DAY HONORS ALL THE PEOPLE
WHO HAVE SERVED OUR COUNTRY IN WARS.

My grandfather fought in World War II, and occasionally he tells stories about being in Germany and helping to free people from the concentration camps. He was shot at and led his company as a captain. I'm so glad he lived through it. I can't quite imagine how frightening and horrible the experience must have been. When I think about those people in the camps being rescued, I think about what heroes the men were who braved their lives to fight Hitler.

There have been so many wars, big ones and small ones. And every war is full of heroes, many of them completely unknown. It's good that there's a day to remember these heroes.

Writing exercise: I'm going to write a card to my grandfather and tell him how much I admire his bravery and the part he played in history.

CHANCE GIFT, MY BREATH
WHY WERE YOU GIVEN TO ME?
–ALEXANDER PUSHKIN

The word breath comes from the same Hebrew root word as wind and spirit. Our breath is the essence of life. When we no longer breathe, we die. Eastern religions often focus on breathing in meditation. Breathe in light, energy and hope. Breathe out the worries of the day.

When my mom is angry, she takes ten slow breaths before she says or does anything. When I'm scared or nervous, I take a couple minutes just to breathe deeply and slowly. This simple act always calms me. I like to think of my breath as a small spiritual wind blowing through me. My breathing connects me to much larger rhythms at work in our universe.

When I need to reflect or relax, I can
always take a few moments to pay attention
to my body breathing in, breathing out.

LIFT UP YOUR EYES UPON
THIS DAY BREAKING FOR YOU.
GIVE BIRTH AGAIN
TO THE DREAM.
—MAYA ANGELOU

I have two girl cousins in their twenties. One has dreams and the other doesn't. The difference is remarkable. The one with dreams is a dancer and has been since she was a little girl. She's always been working her way up in the dance world and always has her next goal in front of her. She consistently practices, almost daily, every week, all year. I wonder if it's because she's so disciplined that she is also a great student. She's graduated from college and now makes a living performing with a dance troupe. She also has ideas and credentials for other career options, should she ever want to get out of dance.

My other cousin hasn't finished college and keeps changing her mind about what she wants to do for a degree or a job. She is also a less passionate and less lively person.

*Remembering and working toward
my dreams keeps me very alive!*

NO ONE CAN MAKE YOU FEEL INFERIOR
WITHOUT YOUR CONSENT.
–ELEANOR ROOSEVELT

I sometimes hear myself saying, "She makes me feel bad." And it's true that some people seem to set this feeling off in me while others don't. But I do have choices in how to respond: no one can make me feel anything unless I agree to go along with them.

When I feel vulnerable around someone, I have choices: I can stay away from that person; I can reflect on my feelings and learn something about myself; I can stay strong in myself and work on not feeling bad. This last one I may need help with, from a friend or my journal.

I have choices about what to do with my feelings.

THE DEFINING FUNCTION OF THE
ARTIST IS TO CHERISH CONSCIOUSNESS.
–MAX EASTMAN

On this day in 1887, the artist Georgia O'Keefe was born. We have been studying her work in art class this year, plus my mother has been buying me calendars that feature O'Keefe's paintings. I love turning the page and seeing which beautiful flower I will live with for the next month.

Her paintings of flowers are exquisite. Each one cherishes that particular flower: its amazing shades of color and nuances of edge and curve. I can only imagine how peaceful I would feel studying and recreating and living so intimately with flowers. Her artwork slows me down, makes me marvel at the individual beauty in all flowers.

!

Artwork all around me helps me to cherish being alive.

WRITTEN WORDS CAN TOUCH AND HEAL
SOMETIMES BETTER THAN SPOKEN ONES.

One of the most difficult relationships in my life right now is with my mom. Although we occasionally have a good time together, it is so easy for us to get into arguments. I admit that I treat her and talk to her in less than respectful ways sometimes. I get full of pent-up feelings, and sometimes I take them all out on her, maybe because I know she's always going to be there for me.

But I'd like to have a better relationship with her. And lately I've been writing her letters. She sometimes leaves me notes, too. Our love for each other shines through more easily when we write our apologies than when we speak them. Her letters always make me feel loved.

If there's a relationship I'm struggling with,
I can always take time to write a letter of apology,
forgiveness, or invitation to connect.

WE HAVE TWO EARS AND ONLY ONE TONGUE SO
THAT WE WOULD LISTEN MORE AND TALK LESS.
–DIOGENES

My friend Jessica's big complaint about her parents is that they don't listen to her. Sometimes we get so busy at my house, we forget to set aside meeting time, but when we remember, my parents do hear me. My brothers and I have a harder time. My mother often says, "Don't interrupt. Listen to him and then you'll get your turn."

I could pay more attention to this myself, especially with my friends. It's so easy for me to get talking and keep talking. I have to remember how important I feel when I feel heard. This is a gift I can give to my friends and family members simply by asking questions and concentrating on their answers.

My ears are meant for hearing. Let me listen
more closely to the people I care for.

ALL MIXED-UP BEHAVIOR COMES FROM
UNPROCESSED PAIN . . . LEARN TO WRITE
ABOUT PAIN, TO TALK ABOUT IT, TO EXPRESS
IT THROUGH EXERCISE, ART, DANCE OR MUSIC.
–MARY PIPHER

It seems to me there are big pains and little pains in life. There's big pain, like when my grandmother died, or Cassie's dad divorced her mom and left town, or Julia's dad died. Then there's smaller pain: the days I feel like I'm just not good enough; or I didn't pass my skill level test in skating, or my mom and I had a big fight.

I find myself pounding out hard feelings on the piano, expressing sadness in how I skate, or writing all the bad feelings I have in my journal. My aunt says that if you work with your pain and transform it, it gives you wings, and if you don't acknowledge it, it weighs and drags you down.

If there's something painful going on in my life right now, I will pay attention to it by talking with a good friend, writing in my journal, or expressing it through sports or art.

IN THE NOISY CONFUSION OF LIFE,
KEEP PEACE WITH YOUR OWN SOUL.

Sometimes high school feels like a whirlwind. So much is going on! First of all, there are the academic demands, which are intense. Then there are the extracurricular activities which are all fun, but that schedule can also be intense. Then there are all the social dynamics: me and my girlfriends, me and guys, my friends and guys.

Whew! Every day I try to remember to take time to check in with my soul—an inspirational reading, a time to write or draw, playing piano—something quiet and reflective and alone.

I will stay more balanced if I soothe my soul every day.

WHY HELP TO MAKE THE WORLD A DREARY PLACE?
WHY BE A RAINY DAY?

Last week, I rode the city bus downtown to help out at my dad's office. I took the bus twice. On the first bus, the driver was unbelievably crabby. His voice was sharp when he answered questions, and if anyone was slow putting their money in the slot, he barked at them. The whole atmosphere of the bus was unpleasant and tense. I couldn't wait to get off.

The next time I rode the bus, I got a friendly driver. He was helpful and gentle and patient. Everyone responded with smiles and jokes. The ride was a pleasure. The contrast between the two made me realize how important the kind of energy I put out into the world is. And how it affects the people around me.

*A smile and pleasant look from me are
easy ways to brighten the world.*

KEEP HOLY THE SABBATH DAY.

In the Genesis book of the bible, God creates some part of our universe every day for six days, and then on the seventh day, God rests. In most Christian traditions, Sunday is the day to rest, slow down, and worship. In the Jewish tradition, the Sabbath begins at sundown on Friday and ends at sundown on Saturday.

The Sabbath, the day of rest, is meant to be a time of renewal and reflection. It's one day each week to look at one's life. All monastic orders have special and regular days set aside for reflection. In my busy life, I like to take some part of my weekend to slow down, to dip deep into the pool of my life instead of busily skittering across its surface.

Every weekend, I need to set aside some time for reflection or worship. A time of rest renews me.

CELEBRATE A PART OF YOUR BODY THAT HAS BEEN CRITICIZED BY SOMEONE ELSE. OPEN YOURSELF UP TO COMPLIMENTS ABOUT THIS BODY PART. LET LOVE TRANSFORM AND MEND YOUR RELATIONSHIP WITH YOUR BODY.
–CARMEN RENEE BERRY

My mom told me a story the other day about how the boys in her eighth grade made fun of her for being flat-chested. She was slow to develop, just like I have been. The most difficult thing, she says, about that time was she didn't confide in anyone about it. She felt so ashamed and she just cried into her pillow alone at night. Now she thinks that if she had talked to anyone, especially an adult, she would have felt better.

Instead it wasn't until years later, when she was in college, that she outgrew her self-consciousness and felt good about her breasts. If anything like this ever happens to me, I don't have to let the criticism color how I feel about my body. I don't have to wait years to talk about it.

Every part of my body is beautiful and lovable and open for healing.

When you respect yourself
you keep your body clean
You walk tall, walk gentle,
don't have to be mean.
–Saundra Sharp

This idea of respect keeps coming up. Respect myself. Respect others. In the dictionary, respect means to give attention or consideration to, to have regard for.

To give attention and consideration to myself, I need to listen to my body and take time to know what my feelings and concerns are. To have regard for is to honor these feelings and concerns by expressing them in some way. I honor what my body is telling me by listening and then taking care of it through rest, good food, or a back rub from Mom.

As I learn how to do these things for myself, I can also give others in my life attention, consideration, and regard.

BEHOLD THE BEAUTY OF A TREE.
FEEL HOW FIRM AND TOUGH IT IS.
SHAKE HANDS WITH THE BRANCHES.
KISS THE LEAVES. DON'T BE EMBARRASSED.
TREES HAVE SEEN IT ALL.
–LINDA GOSS

At our cabin, there is a weeping willow tree down by the water's edge. It is so lovely the way the long, green flowing branches dip and sway in the wind and lean down, as if wanting to caress the earth. After last year's near-tornado, this tree still stands, the trunk as strong and rooted as ever.

Every summer when we return to this place, I go down to visit the willow, and it's like greeting an old friend. Sitting beneath it, I feel happy and comforted. In spite of the whirlwind changes of my life, the tree is still there, its branches blowing and dancing in the summer breeze.

*I would like to be as graceful and sturdy
as my favorite willow tree.*

THANKS, THANK YOU, THANKFULNESS, GRATEFULNESS, GRATITUDE.

I read somewhere that Oprah Winfrey recommends keeping a gratitude journal in which you write down what you're grateful for every day. I've been trying to do this more lately. I take time to see the good things, instead of focusing on what's hard in my life.

Thanksgiving Day, I think, should be less about pilgrims and turkeys and more about being thankful for all the good things and people in our lives. An attitude of gratitude makes it easier to smile and notice the brighter side of life.

Writing exercise: This Thanksgiving week, I will write several pages in my journal about what I'm grateful for.

COMPARING MYSELF TO OTHERS
WHITTLES AWAY AT MY SOUL.

Yesterday I had a bad day. I was feeling a little off, and then I started feeling inferior to all of my friends. Shaiwan is skinnier and talks to boys so easily and naturally. Lindsay is so smart, and she always comes up with great ideas for her research papers. Tess writes better poems than I do. I could go on and on.

But the main problem is that I was feeling off. That's when I am most susceptible to ragging on myself or putting others down in order to feel better myself. Neither one feels very good. Last night, I lit a candle, cried a bit, and wrote in my journal. And I vowed to start over again being me . . . being okay with who I am today.

If I feel smaller and smaller from comparing myself to others, then it's time to look inside and heal what's going on in there.

BEAUTY IS THAT WHICH ATTRACTS YOUR SOUL AND
THAT WHICH LOVES TO GIVE AND NOT TO RECEIVE.
–KAHLIL GIBRAN

On my way home from my bus stop the other day, I
looked up at the sunset spreading itself across the sky.
There were streaks of rose-tinged golden clouds taper-
ing off into threads of violet. It was so beautiful that I
gasped out loud and stood still. I often miss the sunset,
but I was so happy to have noticed this one. It lifted my
heart, gave my mood wings.

There is so much beauty on this earth. Gifts wait for
us to notice and pay attention to them every day, asking
nothing in return.

*Writing exercise: I will write about what
beauty has attracted my soul today.*

NOTHING SPOILS THE TASTE OF PEANUT
BUTTER LIKE UNREQUITED LOVE.
–CHARLIE BROWN

I love this saying because it makes me think of cute little Charlie Brown, because it makes me laugh, and because it's so true. I think we all loved Charlie Brown for his unending and unfulfilled desire. All of us have loved someone who didn't love us back.

My mom agrees. So does my dad. Perhaps it's just part of the human experience, a humbling part. But it sure does ruin the appetite, at least for a time.

If I'm struggling with unrequited love,
I can know that I'm in good company.

I TELL YOU, EVEN ROCKS CRACK, . . .
AND SUDDENLY THE ROCK HAS AN OPEN WOUND.
–DAHLIA RAVIKOVITCH

We all are split open from time to time. Sometimes it's the heartache of love gone bad. Sometimes it's the difficulty of death, like when Julia's dad died. Sometimes it's the pain of a family member's alcoholism or divorce or abusiveness.

We crack open and the wound hurts. But fresh air helps heal wounds. So if we air our wounds, bring them into the open, care for them, we will heal faster. Much of life seems to be a process of healing and of mending as we grow.

I hope to be open to healing on the
days when I feel wounded.

WHY WE TELL STORIES. . .
BECAUSE THE STORY OF OUR LIFE BECOMES OUR LIFE.
–LISEL MUELLER

One of the girls in our class wrote a paper about what it's like to have two moms and no dad. It was funny and poignant at the same time. Another girl wrote about being adopted and all the questions she has for her birth mother. Her paper made me cry.

We traded some of these papers and read sections aloud to each other. It was fascinating and heartwarming, because when I hear these stories, judgment goes out the window. I suddenly see how human everyone is, how each of us struggles with something, and how many different and fascinating lives we lead.

*Telling a story, writing a story, listening to a story
are all important parts of our human community.*

December

THERE'S AN ENORMOUS COMFORT KNOWING
WE ALL LIVE UNDER THIS SAME SKY
WHETHER IN NEW YORK OR DHAKA
WE SEE THE SAME SUN AND SAME MOON.
–ZIA HYDER

In tenth grade we did pen pal exchanges with teenagers in Africa. It made that part of the world seem so much closer and connected to me.

Last summer we took a long trip and ended up 2,000 miles from home. And when I gazed up at the full moon, I knew my friends back home were looking at the same moon and that it appeared just as close to them as it did to me.

All over this planet, people are turning to the moon for gentle splendor and to the sun for warmth on their skin. People with all colors of skin, people speaking hundreds of different languages, people shivering with the cold or sweating under the heat. There is comfort in this sharing.

Writing exercise: Borrowing the first two lines of this poem, I will write my own version of who I share the sky with and what kind of feeling this gives me.

FRIENDS ARE ANGELS WHO LIFT YOU OFF YOUR FEET
WHEN YOUR OWN WINGS HAVE FORGOTTEN HOW TO FLY.

It's true that my friends help me feel better. When I made the team and Jessica patted me on the back and hugged me, it made me even happier than I already was. When my dad was really sick for a month last year, my friends asked me every day how I was doing and sometimes sent cards to my dad as well. If I'm banging around in my room, doing homework, feeling lonely for no really good reason, a short phone call from a friend sends the lonely feelings flying like clouds in the wind.

I am grateful for how my friends warm and lift up my life. When I'm happy for their accomplishments, thoughtful about calling to say hi, or there for them when they are down, I give them the same gift.

Friendship is a gift my heart receives and gives.
I honor this gift, for it gives my heart wings.

WHEN YOU RESPECT YOURSELF YOU COME TO UNDERSTAND
THAT YOUR BODY IS A TEMPLE FOR A NATURAL PLAN,
IT'S AGAINST THAT PLAN TO USE DRUGS OR DOPE—
USE YOUR HEART AND YOUR MIND WHEN YOU NEED TO COPE.
—SAUNDRA SHARP

These lines are from a rap poem called "It's the Law." If I read it over and over, the rhythm of it goes way inside me. The respect yourself rhythm. The body is a temple rhythm. The coping problem.

Sometimes there's a lot to cope with: around me today are a classmate who last month tried to kill herself; my friend whose dad died last year; a few broken hearts because of boyfriends. But I love the idea of using my heart and mind to cope, of my body having a natural plan.

*When there's a lot to cope with, my
heart and mind can find a way.*

[TREES] WERE HERE BEFORE WE WERE.
AND IF THEY EVER DISAPPEAR FROM THE
FACE OF THE EARTH, WHAT HOPE OR BELIEF
WILL HUMANKIND HAVE THEN?
–LINDA GOSS

The tree of love gives shade to all. The tree won't reject your love. I have a favorite tree in my yard. It is a huge beautiful oak tree. In the summer it is lush and full because it has so many branches and leaves. And in the fall it turns glorious colors. This time of year, I love the designs its dark branches make against the winter sky.

This tree has always been like a confidant to me. I can talk to the oak about anything: boys, a fight with a friend, my parents. It's right outside my bedroom window. When I climb up to its first huge branch, I love the solid feel of the bark under my skin. Not only has this old tree witnessed a century's worth of changes, it's been around and steady through all of my life.

Writing exercise: I will take time today to describe my favorite tree, ask it questions, and listen to its answers.

WHEN I RUN
I LAUGH WITH MY LEGS.
–ANNA SWIR

Laughter, they say, heals better than medicine. I recently learned in health class that laughter and exercise release endorphins. I like to think of endorphins as happy blood cells dancing through the blood stream.

I have always loved running. I can remember being five years old and racing barefoot across grassy parks and fields, the wind blowing through my hair. It always made me feel happy. So does skiing. Some of my friends prefer walking or dancing. But I think we all have something we love to do–a way of moving our bodies as a form of laughter.

*I think I'll go ski soon and imagine my
legs happy and laughing as I go.*

THERE'S A DEEP MURMUR UNRAVELED,
THE AIR IS A SONG OF FEATHER,
A SOFT BABBLE OF GRASS. . . .
THERE'S THIS NEED, LIKE A BABY'S, TO BE LOVED.
–ALINE PETTERSSON

I think whenever I feel unloved, I am vulnerable to danger. I watched Cassie go through a period of feeling unloved after her dad left. For a while she talked about it, and then she just got quiet. She started hanging out with Sam, which seemed to help her at first. But then she got real quiet again and didn't spend time with anybody but Sam.

When Sam broke up with her, Lindsay invited her to go horseback riding. Cassie used to ride but had given it up. With Lindsay's help, she got back into it and gradually became that old happy friend again. I think the horse saved her. She felt loved by that horse, and she loved riding it. It was a clean love, unlike the complicated love her family life had become.

*When I feel unloved, I hope I can turn
to healthy ways of feeling loved: asking for
a hug or nuzzling with my favorite animal.*

BUT THE CAT
ONLY THE CAT
TURNED OUT FINISHED,
AND PROUD:
BORN IN A STATE OF TOTAL COMPLETION,
IT STICKS TO ITSELF AND KNOWS EXACTLY WHAT IT WANTS.
–PABLO NERUDA

We have cats at our house. Gita has a huge golden lab. We both love our animals and cuddle with them every day. Lindsay does a lot of horseback riding with her sister–they compete in shows all the time. And Shaiwan has a bunny. We all talk about these animals as if they were members of the family. And they really are. Each animal has its own personality.

Then there are the other animals I admire: the eagle that seems to fly in and out of my dreams, the wolves my aunt is into tracking and reading about. My aunt is into wolves, she thinks, because she is in a period of her life when she needs to be fierce. They are like her guides.

I

Writing exercise: I will think about an animal in my life or my dreams and write about what it symbolizes for me. What do I admire about it, what does it have to teach me?

THERE IS SOMETHING ELSE TO REMEMBER—THAT THIS KIND
OF LOVE BEGINS AT HOME. WE CANNOT GIVE TO THE
OUTSIDE WHAT WE DON'T HAVE ON THE INSIDE.
IF I CAN'T SEE GOD'S LOVE IN MY BROTHER AND SISTER,
THEN HOW CAN I SEE THAT LOVE IN SOMEBODY ELSE?
–MOTHER TERESA

I often get caught up in big ideas: become a generous soul like Mother Teresa, prepare to travel to India and help the most downtrodden on the streets of Calcutta. Sounds important and exotic, doesn't it?

Yet it's hard for me to see that my brother is feeling down and that I could be extra kind to him. My mom has to nudge me on these things, and even then I sometimes resist. I don't know why. What's so hard about showing a little love and affection when my brother is feeling sick or has had a bad day?

*Let me start my improve-the-world
program right at home with my family.*

LANGUAGE IS THE BLOOD OF THE SOUL INTO WHICH
THOUGHTS RUN AND OUT OF WHICH THEY GROW.
–Oliver Wendell Holmes, Sr.

Sometimes I like to think about words, about how strange life would be without them. I wonder about the creation of words and languages. So many words, so many languages all over our planet and all across time! Language is how I learn about my world and how I communicate with others. Words can heal and words can hurt.

Every once in a while, I like to spend a day appreciating words. I do this by reading poems, by listening to the words that fall from the mouths of those around me, by thumbing through the dictionary and picking out words that seem to jump out at me, and by writing.

Writing exercise: I'll find a word in the dictionary that I'm not familiar with but that I like the sound of. I'll write about its definition, sound, meaning, soul.

SOME (YOUNG) WOMEN NOTICE THAT THEY
FEEL MORE EMOTIONAL RIGHT BEFORE
AND AT THE BEGINNING OF THEIR PERIOD.
–KAREN AND JENNIFER GRAVELLE

In the last few days, I have burst into tears three times: once during a movie we were watching in English class (embarrassing), once when I let a goal into the soccer net when I was goalie (again, embarrassing), and then when my mother asked me to clean my room. I also snapped at my mother when she picked me up because she was ten minutes late.

Even I was starting to wonder what was going on. Then my period arrived and I remembered. If I'm at all tired or extra-stressed and it's right before my period, I get emotional over things I would ordinarily take in stride. It helps if I keep track of my cycle and sort of know when to expect this. It also helps if I get a little extra rest or nurturing and eat especially healthy during this time.

In life's ups and downs, there are a few things I can plan ahead for. It's a way of taking care of myself.

SOMETIMES FRIENDS JUST WANT TO VENT,
AND DON'T NEED YOU TO SOLVE THEIR PROBLEMS . . .
THIS IS YOUR CHANCE TO OFFER SISTERLY SUPPORT,
NOT BRAINY ADVICE.
—MINDY MORGENSTERN

We did an exercise in health class on the importance of listening. We had to take turns, and when it was my turn to listen, I could say nothing. That was hard: I could feel exactly how often I have the impulse to interrupt.

When it was my turn to be heard, it felt so good. I talked for a period of time just about me, and my partner listened and responded. She did not speak except to say back to me what she was hearing. I realized how seldom the focus stays on me and how good it feels to be truly listened to.

Part of being a good friend is listening to my friends, truly listening. I can keep getting better and better at this.

> IF YOU HAVE HURT SOMEONE ELSE, ASK THAT PERSON
> ONE MORE QUESTION, 'HOW CAN I MAKE AMENDS?'
> –CARMEN RENEE BERRY

I got carried away the other day and mentioned to Kevin that he ought to ask Cassie to the dance. She was so mad at me! She likes him, but she was mortified that I had said anything. She wants him to ask her only if he wants to, not because I made him feel like he should.

At first I wanted to shrug my shoulders and say "Whatever." But when I thought more about it, I realized I needed to be more respectful of Cassie. So I apologized and asked what I could do to mend things. She said I should keep quiet next time and now that Kevin had asked her to the dance, she would appreciate it if I did not take credit for it. Okay.

I guess I will make mistakes and hurt my friends from time to time. But when I sincerely want to make amends, there is almost always a way to do so.

> I BEGAN WRITING POEMS,
> . . . SOON AFTER MY MOTHER DIED
> . . . PLACED MY GRIEF
> IN THE MOUTH OF LANGUAGE
> THE ONLY THING THAT WOULD GRIEVE WITH ME.
> –LISEL MUELLER

My parents are back together again now, and it seems to be going okay, thank God. But when they were separated and I was afraid they were moving toward the big D word (Divorce), I felt such sadness and grief. It made me realize how painful it's probably been for Cassie, whose parent divorced a year ago. She said it was like an earthquake rumbled through her house and split it in two. She still often feels split in two.

I guess we can all heal, and we all have scars. But I noticed during this time how much writing helped me. It let loose the many bottled-up feelings and worries I had. On paper, it all seemed more manageable, even beautiful at times.

Writing exercise: I'll explore something causing me grief or sadness. I'll describe it and turn it into a poem.

FAMILIES COME IN ALL SHAPES AND SIZES.

During that period when my dad moved out of the house, I felt so self-conscious about my family life. I felt different, as if there was something wrong with us as a family. This translated into there being something wrong with me.

Many of my friends have unique family situations and, although these seem fine to me, I wonder if they struggle with feeling different. Amy has two moms–her mom is gay, and her father dropped out of the picture long ago. Ellie's mom is a single parent. Teresa lives mostly with her dad. Lizzie's family has six kids, which is different in its own way! After my experience, I've become more sensitive to other people's situations. I'm more open about telling them what's cool about their unique family. They always appreciate it.

I hope I can always be sensitive to and
supportive of my friends' family life.

DON'T BREAK MY HEART . . .

I dreaded it happening to me. I was crazy about Brian and could have hung out with him much longer. We did a lot together for about three months, and then he told me he wanted to end it. What could I say? I was devastated. When he dropped me off that day, I walked slowly into the house and straight up to my room, where I cried into my pillow for hours.

For the next few weeks I was pretty low. Lizzie and Cassie stayed close and kept telling me they understood and that it would get better. They were a comfort. After a month had passed, I went on a weekend retreat with my church. We actually did an exercise for healing broken hearts. I guess opening my heart to love opens my heart to being hurt. But now I know my hurts can heal, and I'd rather live my life with an open heart.

Heartbreak is part of being human.
Friendships and hot baths and time help heal me.

LIFE GIVES LIFE
AND IT'S NO GREAT COST
SO EAT, SING,
OFFER THIS LIFE OF EARTH
BACK TO EARTH.
–LINDA HOGAN

Ever since I was little, I've been helping my parents with the garden. We have a small vegetable garden and a bigger flower garden. Planting is a way to give back to this earth. I plant a bulb and when I do, I express faith in the magic of dirt and earth.

When we went to the park and found lots of cans and litter left from a party, my friends and I cleaned it up. That's another way of giving back to this earth. Eating and singing with joy are also ways of honoring and celebrating this earth.

Writing exercise: How do I give life back to this earth?

THINK OF YOURSELF AS AN INCANDESCENT POWER,
ILLUMINATED AND PERHAPS FOREVER TALKED
TO BY GOD AND HIS MESSENGERS.
–BRENDA UELAND

I looked up incandescent in the dictionary and it said, "glowing, brightly shining, brilliantly luminous." When we're at our cabin, the sun shines across the lake and dapples its way through the green leaves where it lights up my east-facing window. This makes me feel so alive, so happy.

That light is the image that comes to me when I think of an incandescent, a brightly shining, power. When I feel the energy of a great and kind spirit shining into and through me, my eyes probably do glow brighter. I like to think of myself as filled with light, especially when I remember that I am luminous when I'm in touch with forces greater than myself.

I can let the light of love shine through me.

IN ORDER TO MAKE PEACE WITH OUR BODIES, WE CANNOT SIMPLY ACCEPT THE DEFINITIONS OF BEAUTY GIVEN TO US BY OUR SOCIETY, BECAUSE THESE STANDARDS ARE ARBITRARY AND IMPOSSIBLE TO MEET.
–CARMEN RENEE BERRY

On a day when I've seen too many commercials or picked up too many magazines displaying skinny models, I'm vulnerable. Vulnerable to drooling over the model's body and to finding endless things wrong with mine.

Then my friend Shaiwan will say to me, "Girl, you look great today. That color blue is too good to be true on you." Or I'll remember my mom saying to me after the band concert, "You looked so beautiful and radiant up on that stage!" Why waste my time wanting the impossible in terms of looks? Why not appreciate and even approve of my body? It's beautiful in its own way!

Loving life and accepting my body work together to make an attractive and distinctive-looking me!

SLOW DOWN AND ENJOY LIFE. IT'S NOT ONLY THE
SCENERY YOU MISS BY GOING TOO FAST—YOU ALSO MISS
THE SENSE OF WHERE YOU ARE GOING AND WHY.
–EDDIE CANTOR

Everyone I know leads a pretty busy life. My friends have school plus lots of activities. Most of us do something for money—either baby-sitting or some other job. I've noticed that life is better for me if I balance all this busyness with some down time. If I have a really busy week, then maybe I need to plan to spend one weekend night at home.

At some point in a hectic weekend, I try to play the piano for a while or sit on the couch and read a book. Both tend to calm and slow me down. This time seems to re-energize me, but it also helps me to see my life more clearly. Small but important thoughts surface during these quiet times.

*I need to remember that I'm always grateful
for the insights I receive when I slow down.*

I HAD TO STOP TALKING FOR NEARLY A YEAR.
THEN I MET, OR RATHER GOT TO KNOW,
THE LADY WHO THREW ME MY FIRST LIFELINE.
–MAYA ANGELOU

Maya Angelou, now a prize-winning, famous, and highly respected writer, quit speaking for a year. She did so in response to the trauma of rape. My friend Tess lost her father to suicide. It was so shocking and she felt so ashamed that she couldn't sing for a year. She's always had a beautiful singing voice, but she just couldn't use it.

In Maya Angelou's case, a woman in the neighborhood took a special liking to her. To converse with her, Maya began to talk. Tess sang for the first time at my birthday party. We were all good friends gathered together, and out of the blue she began to sing in her beautiful voice. We all knew what a breakthrough it was, and we felt honored that it was in the safe harbor of our friendships that her voice first set sail..

If I am ever rendered voiceless or am silenced in some way, I will listen for the sounds of special friendships.

WINTER SOLSTICE MARKS THE SHORTEST DAY
OF THE YEAR IN THE NORTHERN HEMISPHERE.

The light faded fast from the sky today. School's out
for the holidays, and to celebrate the solstice my dad
built a big fire outside. My parents and some friends and
I all stood around the flames. We wrote on pieces of
paper what dark parts of ourselves we want to burn
away and what we want to bring into the light. Some of
us read aloud what we wrote, others didn't. Even the
silent ones threw their darkness and dreams into the
fire. We watched them all curl up and burn, one at a
time.

My mom wanted to burn her impatience and re-
ignite her love of playing the piano. Shaiwan wanted to
burn her tendency to think she's not good enough and
light up her love of dancing again.

*Writing exercise: On this darkest of days, I will light a can-
dle, write about the dark parts of myself I'd like to let go of,
and the parts of me that want to dance more in the light.*

WITHIN OUR LONG, VARIED (JEWISH) TRADITION
WE FOUND MANY WAYS TO CELEBRATE, WORSHIP,
AND SEARCH FOR GOD IN THE UNIVERSE,
IN HUMANITY, AND IN OURSELVES.
–RUTH BRIN

Hanukkah's date changes every year because it is based on the lunar calendar, but the holiday usually falls during this week. It lasts eight days, which are symbolized by the menorah or candle-holder. There is a candle for each of the eight days and a helper candle for lighting them all. During this celebration, candles are lit, a special oil is used, and food is a dancing feast.

The candles are lit in memory of the rededication of the temple in Jerusalem over two thousand years ago. Those little twinkling lights in people's living room windows honor the survival of the Jews, who have overcome huge wars and much persecution.

!

*Help me to remember the people who
celebrate Hanukkah and to remember, honor,
and borrow from the richness of their traditions.*

WHY SHOULD WE ALL USE OUR CREATIVE POWER?
BECAUSE THERE IS NOTHING THAT MAKES PEOPLE
SO GENEROUS, JOYFUL, LIVELY, BOLD AND
COMPASSIONATE, SO INDIFFERENT TO FIGHTING
AND THE ACCUMULATION OF OBJECTS AND MONEY.
–BRENDA UELAND

There's a humanities teacher at my school who is very popular. She is always encouraging students to figure out what their passions are and to move toward them. She believes in creativity in all forms and seems to bring out the creative energy in her students.

She has more vitality than most adults I know. With wild hair and colorful clothing, she reminds me of the Magic School Bus teacher, Ms. Frizzle. Write poems, she says, play music, dance! Discover what you love and immerse yourself in it. Create! Create! Create!

I'd rather live a life that is passionate and creative than one that is tied to acquiring things.

'TWAS THE NIGHT BEFORE CHRISTMAS
WHEN ALL THROUGH THE HOUSE
NOT A CREATURE WAS STIRRING,
NOT EVEN A MOUSE.

I love the night before Christmas, when all the busy-ness of getting ready for Christmas seems to subside. My family and I go to church, and we sing the carols I love to sing. We sing about angels and love, and the music touches me and the church is so beautiful with deep green branches and bright red poinsettias all around.

And on our drive home, we take the slow route so we can ooh and aah over Christmas lights on people's houses. Those lights make me cheerful and light up these darkest months in simple and festive ways. In bed at night I feel a peaceful, expectant hush settle over the house, and I always have good dreams.

*Writing exercise: I will describe
Christmas Eve, for it is a special day.*

THEN PEALED THE BELLS MORE LOUD AND DEEP:
GOD IS NOT DEAD, NOR DOTH HE SLEEP;
THE WRONG SHALL FAIL, THE RIGHT PREVAIL,
WITH PEACE ON EARTH,
GOOD WILL TO MEN.
–HENRY WADSWORTH LONGFELLOW

We took my little brother's new sled to the sledding hill today. A fresh layer of six inches of snow fell last night. It was magical! A couple of other families were out around noon: between church in the morning, present opening, and afternoon dinners. The church bells were ringing, and they sounded so lovely. I stood on the hill and thought about how bells rang like that hundreds of years ago. All these years, bells have rung to mark special days and events or to warn people of danger.

I took a flying slide down that hill and the timeless and incredibly hopeful sound of the bells tolled around me. The snow felt smooth beneath my sled and the winter wind chilled made my face. I felt happy.

Writing exercise: I will write about how the world slows down on this day. What sights, sounds, and feelings do I notice in the quiet slowness?

EVERY BLADE OF GRASS HAS ITS ANGEL THAT BENDS
OVER IT AND WHISPERS, "GROW, GROW."
–TALMUD

So, here is this ancient book, talking about angels. I
thought maybe talk about angels was more of a current
trend, but it seems they have been around forever. If
every living thing has an angel chanting over it "Grow,
grow," then perhaps I should count on mine more often.

My aunt thinks that my uncle, the pilot, has a special
angel with him. I've been saying a prayer to my
guardian angel since I was about four. My mom says that
sometimes if she's worried about me, she'll ask my angel
to take care of me.

Around me, around all of us, is an
angel whispering, "Grow, grow."

THE DEAL IS, OUR BROTHERS AND SISTERS
WILL BE WITH US (HOPEFULLY) LONG AFTER OUR
PARENTS ARE GONE. . . . STUDIES HAVE SHOWN THAT
PEOPLE WHO HAVE CLOSE RELATIONSHIPS WITH THEIR
SIBLINGS LIVE LONGER, HAPPIER, HEALTHIER LIVES.
—MINDY MORGENSTERN

When I went away to camp last summer, I was shocked at how much I missed my brothers. I missed my older brother because he is actually becoming someone I can talk and joke with. And I missed my pesky little brother's sweet face and big blue eyes and the way he looks adoringly at me whenever I'm nice to him.

There's no one in the world I fight with more than my brothers, but ever since going to camp, I do appreciate them. I try to be less mean and more affectionate. I try to appreciate them without having to go away to feel that way. After all, maybe I'm investing in living a longer, happier life. Some days I do better than others.

Writing exercise: What do I really love and cherish about my siblings? What would I miss the most if anything happened to either of them?

I SHUT MY EYES IN ORDER TO SEE.
–Paul Gauguin

Isn't it interesting that this world-famous painter closed his eyes to see?

Lately, when I'm confused or struggling to get clear about something, I sit with my eyes closed for a while. It's amazing how relaxed I feel after just a few minutes. Then when I'm relaxed I begin to think more clearly. When I'm tight in my body and anxiously going over a problem again and again, I only get more confused.

So this thing about closing eyes in order to see is beginning to make sense. It's like learning to see with our insides, our hearts, our souls.

*Writing exercise: I will describe what
I see today when I close my eyes.*

DEVELOP INTERESTS IN LIFE AS YOU SEE IT; IN PEOPLE, THINGS, LITERATURE, MUSIC—THE WORLD IS SO RICH, SIMPLY THROBBING WITH RICH TREASURES, BEAUTIFUL SOULS AND INTERESTING PEOPLE. FORGET YOURSELF.
–HENRY MILLER

Every once in a while I catch myself saying I'm bored. That usually means I'm tired. Because I can always go to my bookshelf and read or reread a great book. I can always go to the piano and bang out whatever kind of mood I'm in. I can get out my watercolors or special chalks and paint or draw. I can hop on my bike and ride by beautiful lakes and trees.

I can listen to great music on my CD or plan a gala evening at the theater or a concert hall.

The world is an amazing place, full of amazing people.
All I need to enter into this richness is an open heart.

LIFE IS FOR LIVING SO LIVE IT BIG AND TO THE FULLEST.
–Mindy Morgenstern

I had two opposite days this week. One day I got off on the wrong track and felt self-conscious and shy and like I should hide myself all day. The next morning, my dad told me I had been accepted into the music camp I've been trying to get into for years. It got me so jazzed up that I went to school and asked every question I felt like asking, talked to every boy and girl I felt like talking to, asked for special help from my teacher. I was out there–on the proverbial limb–all day. And it felt so good.

Adventuring out into the world by going to music camp and canoeing camp feels great, too. I think living fully means loving life and the people in my life with enthusiasm.

Writing exercise: What are the specific ways I love life to its fullest? For contrast, what are some ways I narrow my life?

DANCE AND YOU'LL LOVE YOUR BODY.

At a family wedding last summer, I watched my over-weight aunt dance. She could move her body so smoothly and with such fluidity that I didn't even notice her weight. Instead, I noticed her gracefulness.

Sometimes if I'm feeling down about my body, I will shut the door to my room, light a candle, and dance in front of the mirror. Once I feel my body in motion, it feels good. I see my arms, legs, and torso moving as fluid parts of a graceful whole, and I cannot help liking my body again. Dancing is always a good way to regain my sense of body-acceptance, even body-celebration.

*It's New Year's Eve! Whether I dance alone,
with my girlfriends, or with a special guy, let me
celebrate the year's end with my heart, body, and soul!*

PATRICIA HOOLIHAN is the author of *Small Miracles: Daily Meditations for Mothers in Recovery* (Bantam). She also co-authored *Today's Gift*, a meditation book (Hazelden) and wrote *Family Attitudes*, and *The Step Dance: Ins and Outs of Stepparenting* (Hazelden). Ms. Hoolihan lives with her family in Minneapolis, Minnesota.